EUROPEAN POLITICAL, ECONOMIC, AND SECURITY ISSUES

DEMOCRATIC CREDENTIALS OF THE EUROPEAN UNION

BACKGROUND AND ANALYSIS

EUROPEAN POLITICAL, ECONOMIC, AND SECURITY ISSUES

Additional books in this series can be found on Nova's website under the Series tab.

Additional e-books in this series can be found on Nova's website under the e-book tab.

European Political, Economic, and Security Issues

Democratic Credentials of the European Union

Background and Analysis

Evonne Graham
Editor

New York

Copyright © 2014 by Nova Science Publishers, Inc.

All rights reserved. No part of this book may be reproduced, stored in a retrieval system or transmitted in any form or by any means: electronic, electrostatic, magnetic, tape, mechanical photocopying, recording or otherwise without the written permission of the Publisher.

For permission to use material from this book please contact us:
Telephone 631-231-7269; Fax 631-231-8175
Web Site: http://www.novapublishers.com

NOTICE TO THE READER

The Publisher has taken reasonable care in the preparation of this book, but makes no expressed or implied warranty of any kind and assumes no responsibility for any errors or omissions. No liability is assumed for incidental or consequential damages in connection with or arising out of information contained in this book. The Publisher shall not be liable for any special, consequential, or exemplary damages resulting, in whole or in part, from the readers' use of, or reliance upon, this material. Any parts of this book based on government reports are so indicated and copyright is claimed for those parts to the extent applicable to compilations of such works.

Independent verification should be sought for any data, advice or recommendations contained in this book. In addition, no responsibility is assumed by the publisher for any injury and/or damage to persons or property arising from any methods, products, instructions, ideas or otherwise contained in this publication.

This publication is designed to provide accurate and authoritative information with regard to the subject matter covered herein. It is sold with the clear understanding that the Publisher is not engaged in rendering legal or any other professional services. If legal or any other expert assistance is required, the services of a competent person should be sought. FROM A DECLARATION OF PARTICIPANTS JOINTLY ADOPTED BY A COMMITTEE OF THE AMERICAN BAR ASSOCIATION AND A COMMITTEE OF PUBLISHERS.

Additional color graphics may be available in the e-book version of this book.

Library of Congress Cataloging-in-Publication Data

ISBN: 978-1-63321-628-0

Published by Nova Science Publishers, Inc. † New York

CONTENTS

Preface		**vii**
Chapter 1	The European Union: Questions and Answers *Kristin Archick*	**1**
Chapter 2	The European Parliament *Kristin Archick*	**23**
Chapter 3	The European Union: A Democratic Institution? *Vaughne Miller and Jon Lunn,* *with contributions by Steven Ayres*	**51**
Index		**155**

PREFACE

The European Union (EU) is a political and economic partnership that represents a unique form of cooperation among sovereign countries. The Union is the latest stage in a process of integration begun after World War II, initially by six Western European countries, to foster interdependence and make another war in Europe unthinkable. Today, the EU is composed of 28 member states, including most of the countries of Central and Eastern Europe, and has helped to promote peace, stability, and economic prosperity throughout the European continent. The EU has been built through a series of binding treaties, and over the years, EU member states have sought to harmonize laws and adopt common policies on an increasing number of economic, social, and political issues. EU member states share a customs union, a single market in which goods, people, and capital move freely, a common trade policy, and a common agricultural policy. This book serves as a primer on the EU and provides a brief description of U.S.-EU relations that may be of interest in the 113th Congress. This book also asks questions about the democratic credentials of the European Union.

Chapter 1 – The European Union (EU) is a political and economic partnership, built through a series of binding treaties that represents a unique form of cooperation among sovereign countries. The EU is composed of 28 member states, including most of the countries of Central and Eastern Europe, and has helped to promote peace, stability, and economic prosperity throughout the European continent. The United States and the EU have a dynamic political partnership and share a huge trade and investment relationship. This report serves as a primer on the EU and provides a brief description of U.S.-EU relations that may be of interest to Congress.

Chapter 2 – Between May 22 and May 25, 2014, the 28 member states of the European Union (EU) held elections for the next European Parliament

(EP). The Parliament is a key EU institution that represents the citizens of the EU. It works closely with the two other main EU bodies, the European Commission (the EU's executive) and the Council of the European Union (also known as the Council of Ministers, on which the national governments of the EU's 28 member states are represented). Members of the European Parliament (MEPs) serve five-year terms, and have been directly elected since 1979. The next EP will have 751 seats.

Once limited to being a consultative assembly, the EP has accumulated more power over time. Experts assert that the EU's latest effort at institutional reform—the Lisbon Treaty, which entered into force on December 1, 2009—has increased the relative power of the EP within the EU considerably. The EP now shares legislative power with the Council of Ministers in most policy areas, giving the EP the right to accept, amend, or reject the vast majority of EU laws (with some exceptions in areas such as tax matters or foreign policy). The Lisbon Treaty also gives the EP the power to decide on the allocation of the EU budget jointly with the Council, the right to approve or reject international agreements, and greater decision-making authority on trade-related issues. At the same time, some analysts contend that the EP still lacks the legitimacy of national parliaments and that many European citizens remain unaware of the EP's role within the EU.

Members of the European Parliament (MEPs) are organized into political groups, which caucus according to political ideology rather than nationality. The EP's standing committees are key actors in the adoption of EU legislation, and EP delegations maintain international parliament-toparliament relations. In the upcoming EP elections, anti-EU or "euroskeptic" political parties— which are predominantly nationalistic, populist, and on the far right of the political spectrum, although a few are on the left or far left—appear poised to make moderate to significant gains in several EU countries. As a result, some analysts suggest that they could alter the political composition of the next EP and have implications for the EU's legislative and policymaking processes over the next five years, especially if hardline elements are able to form a new political group. Other experts question the ability of these euroskeptic parties to forge a united front in a way that would significantly affect the functioning and character of the next EP.

The EP has not been shy about exerting its new powers under the Lisbon Treaty, and in some areas, with implications for U.S. interests. For example, EP concerns about U.S. data privacy safeguards have complicated U.S.-EU negotiations in the past on several information-sharing agreements aimed at countering terrorism. Following the initial unauthorized disclosures in June

2013 of U.S. National Security Agency surveillance programs and subsequent allegations that U.S. intelligence agencies have monitored EU diplomatic offices and engaged in other surveillance activities in Europe, many analysts worry about whether future U.S.-EU information-sharing agreements will be able to secure the necessary EP approval. In addition, EP approval will ultimately be required to allow any eventual U.S.-EU agreement on a Transatlantic Trade and Investment Partnership (TTIP) to enter into force.

Ties between the EP and the U.S. Congress are long-standing, and institutional cooperation currently exists through the Transatlantic Legislators' Dialogue (TLD). In light of the EP's growing role as an actor in the conduct of U.S.-EU relations, the EP and its activities may be of increasing interest to the 113th Congress.

Chapter 3 - This paper asks questions about the democratic credentials of the European Union. The paper begins by looking at definitions of democracy and the historical development of democratic political systems. It then looks at the European Union's decision-making institutions and at a range of views from academics and politicians on the extent to which they conform to generally accepted norms of democratic government.

The paper acknowledges the EU's 'democratic deficit' and considers the causes of this. In the context of future EU Treaty reform, it considers possible remedies for the democratic deficit, including those proposed by the UK Government.

In: Democratic Credentials of the European Union   ISBN: 978-1-63321-628-0
Editor: Evonne Graham   © 2014 Nova Science Publishers, Inc.

Chapter 1

THE EUROPEAN UNION: QUESTIONS AND ANSWERS[*]

Kristin Archick

SUMMARY

The European Union (EU) is a political and economic partnership that represents a unique form of cooperation among sovereign countries. The Union is the latest stage in a process of integration begun after World War II, initially by six Western European countries, to foster interdependence and make another war in Europe unthinkable. Today, the EU is composed of 28 member states, including most of the countries of Central and Eastern Europe, and has helped to promote peace, stability, and economic prosperity throughout the European continent.

The EU has been built through a series of binding treaties, and over the years, EU member states have sought to harmonize laws and adopt common policies on an increasing number of economic, social, and political issues. EU member states share a customs union, a single market in which goods, people, and capital move freely, a common trade policy, and a common agricultural policy. Eighteen EU member states use a common currency (the euro). In addition, the EU has been developing a Common Foreign and Security Policy (CFSP), which includes a Common Security and Defense Policy (CSDP), and pursuing cooperation in the

---

[*] This is an edited, reformatted and augmented version of a Congressional Research Service publication, CRS Report for Congress RS21372, prepared for Members and Committees of Congress, from www.crs.gov, dated January 15, 2014.

area of Justice and Home Affairs (JHA) to forge common internal security measures.

EU member states work together through common institutions to set policy and to promote their collective interests. Key EU institutions include the European Council, composed of EU Heads of State or Government, which acts as the strategic guide and driving force for EU policy; the European Commission, which upholds the common interest of the Union as a whole and functions as the EU's executive; the Council of the European Union (also known as the Council of Ministers), which represents the national governments; and the directly elected European Parliament, which represents the citizens of the EU.

EU decision-making processes and the role played by the EU institutions vary depending on the subject under consideration. For most economic and social issues, EU member states have largely pooled their national sovereignty, and EU decision-making has a supranational quality. Decisions in other areas, such as foreign policy, require the unanimous consensus of all 28 member states. The Lisbon Treaty, which took effect in December 2009, is the EU's latest attempt to reform its governing institutions and decision-making processes in order to enable an enlarged EU to function more effectively. The Lisbon Treaty also seeks to give the EU a stronger voice in the foreign policy realm and to increase democratic transparency within the EU.

The United States has strongly supported the European integration project since its inception as a means to foster democratic states and robust trading partners. The United States and the EU have a dynamic political partnership and share a huge trade and investment relationship. To expand and strengthen the transatlantic economy even further, the United States and the EU are pursuing a comprehensive and ambitious Transatlantic Trade and Investment Partnership. Nevertheless, some tensions exist in the relationship, ranging from long-standing U.S.-EU trade disputes to climate change. Data privacy also continues to be a sticking point, especially following the recent allegations of U.S. surveillance activities in Europe.

This report serves as a primer on the EU and provides a brief description of U.S.-EU relations that may be of interest in the 113th Congress.

WHAT IS THE EUROPEAN UNION?

The European Union (EU) is a political and economic partnership that represents a unique form of cooperation among 28 member states.[1] Built through a series of binding treaties, the Union is the latest stage in a process of integration begun after World War II to promote peace and economic prosperity in Europe. Its founders hoped that by creating specified areas in which member states agreed to share sovereignty—initially in coal and steel production, economics and trade, and nuclear energy—it would promote interdependence and make another war in Europe unthinkable. Since the 1950s, this European integration project has expanded to encompass other economic sectors, a customs union, a single market in which goods, people, and capital move freely, a common trade policy, a common agricultural policy, many aspects of social and environmental policy, and a common currency (the euro) that is used by 18 member states. Since the mid-1990s, EU member states have also taken significant steps toward political integration, with decisions to develop a Common Foreign and Security Policy (CFSP) and efforts to promote cooperation in the area of Justice and Home Affairs (JHA), which is aimed at forging common internal security measures.

HOW DOES THE EU WORK?

EU member states work together through common institutions (see next question) to set policy and promote their collective interests. Over the past several decades, EU members have progressively committed to harmonizing laws and adopting joint policies on an extensive and increasing number of issues. However, decision-making processes and the role of the EU institutions vary depending on the subject under consideration.

On a multitude of economic and social policies (previously termed Pillar One, or the European Community), EU members have essentially pooled their sovereignty and EU institutions hold executive authority. Integration in these fields—which range from trade and agriculture to education and the environment—has traditionally been the most developed and far-reaching. EU decisions in such areas often have a supranational quality because most are subject to a complex majority voting system among the member states and are legally binding.

For issues falling under the Common Foreign and Security Policy (once known as Pillar Two), EU member states have agreed to cooperate, but most decision-making is intergovernmental and requires the unanimous agreement of all 28 EU countries. Thus, member states retain more discretion over their participation as any one country can veto a decision. For many years, unanimous agreement among the member states was also largely the rule for policy-making in the Justice and Home Affairs area (formerly Pillar Three);

recently, however, EU member states agreed to accelerate integration in the JHA field by extending the use of the EU's majority voting system to most JHA issues and giving EU institutions a greater role in JHA policy-making.

HOW IS THE EU GOVERNED?

The EU is governed by several institutions. They do not correspond exactly to the traditional branches of government or division of power in representative democracies. Rather, they embody the EU's dual supranational and intergovernmental character:

- The *European Council* acts as the strategic guide for EU policy. It is composed of the Heads of State or Government of the EU's member states and the President of the European Commission; it meets several times a year in what are often termed "EU summits." The European Council is headed by a President, appointed by the member states to organize the Council's work and facilitate consensus.
- The *European Commission* is essentially the EU's executive and upholds the common interest of the EU as a whole. It implements and manages EU decisions and common policies, ensures that the provisions of the EU's treaties and rules are carried out properly, and has the sole right of legislative initiative in most policy areas. It is composed of 28 Commissioners, one from each country, who are appointed by agreement among the member states to five-year terms. One Commissioner serves as Commission President; the others hold distinct portfolios (e.g., agriculture, energy, trade). On many issues, the Commission represents the EU internationally and handles negotiations with outside countries. The Commission is also the EU's primary administrative entity.
- The *Council of the European Union* (also called the *Council of Ministers)* represents the 28 national governments. The Council enacts legislation, usually based on proposals put forward by the Commission, and agreed to (in most cases) by the European Parliament. Different ministers from each country participate in Council meetings depending on the subject under consideration (e.g., foreign ministers would meet to discuss the Middle East, agriculture ministers to discuss farm subsidies). Most decisions are subject to a

complex majority voting system, but some areas—such as foreign and defense policy, taxation, or accepting new members—require unanimity. The Presidency of the Council rotates among the member states, changing every six months; the country holding the Presidency helps set agenda priorities and organizes most of the work of the Council.

- The *European Parliament* represents the citizens of the EU. The Parliament currently consists of 766 members who are directly elected for five-year terms. Each member state has a number of seats roughly proportional to the size of its population. Although the Parliament cannot initiate legislation, it shares legislative power with the Council of Ministers in many policy areas, giving it the right to accept, amend, or reject the majority of proposed EU legislation in a process known as the "ordinary legislative procedure" or "co-decision." The Parliament also decides on the allocation of the EU's budget jointly with the Council. Members of the European Parliament (MEPs) caucus according to political affiliation, rather than nationality.

- A number of other institutions also play key roles in the EU. The *Court of Justice* interprets EU laws and its rulings are binding; a *Court of Auditors* monitors the EU's financial management; the *European Central Bank* manages the euro and EU monetary policy; and a number of *advisory committees* represent economic, social, and regional interests.

WHAT IS THE LISBON TREATY?

On December 1, 2009, the EU's latest institutional reform endeavor—the Lisbon Treaty—came into force following its ratification by all of the EU's then-27 member states. It is the final product of an effort begun in 2002 to reform the EU's governing institutions and decision-making processes in order to enable an enlarged Union to function more effectively. In addition, the treaty seeks to give the EU a stronger and more coherent voice and identity on the world stage, and to increase democracy and transparency within the EU.[2]

To help accomplish these goals, the Lisbon Treaty establishes two new leadership positions. The new President of the European Council, chosen by the member states for a term of two and one-half years (renewable once), now chairs the meetings of the 28 EU Heads of State or Government, serves as coordinator and spokesman for their work, seeks to ensure policy continuity, and strives to forge consensus among the member states. The Lisbon Treaty also created a dual-hatted position of High Representative of the Union for Foreign Affairs and Security Policy to serve essentially as the EU's chief diplomat. The High Representative is both an agent of the Council of Ministers—and thus speaks for the member states on foreign policy issues—as well as a Vice President of the European Commission, responsible for managing most of the Commission's diplomatic activities and foreign assistance programs (see "Does the EU Have a Foreign Policy?" for more information).

Among other key measures, the Lisbon Treaty simplifies the EU's qualified majority voting system and expands its use to policy areas previously subject to member state unanimity in the Council of Ministers; this change was intended in part to speed EU decision-making and improve its efficiency. Nevertheless, in practice, member states will likely still strive for consensus on sensitive policy issues (such as police cooperation, immigration, and countering terrorism) that are usually viewed as central to a nation-state's sovereignty. At the same time, the mere possibility of a vote may make member state governments more willing to compromise and reach a common policy decision.

In addition, the Lisbon Treaty increases the relative power of the European Parliament in an effort to improve democratic accountability. It strengthens the Parliament's role in the EU's budgetary process and extends the use of the "co-decision" procedure to more policy areas, including agriculture and home affairs issues.[3]

As such, the treaty gives the Parliament a say equal to that of the member states in the Council of Ministers over the vast majority of EU legislation (with some exceptions, such as most aspects of foreign and defense policy). In addition, the Lisbon Treaty provides national parliaments with a degree of greater authority to challenge draft EU legislation and allows for the possibility of new legislative proposals based on citizen initiatives.

Key EU Positions and Current Leaders

The *President of the European Council* is Herman Van Rompuy, a former prime minister of Belgium. Appointed by the member states in 2009 initially, Van Rompuy is the first holder of this new position, which was created by the Lisbon Treaty. In June 2012, Van Rompuy was re-appointed to a second term, which will conclude in November 2014.

The *President of the European Commission* is José Manuel Barroso, a former prime minister of Portugal. Barroso has served as Commission President since 2004, and is currently in his second five-year term, which will end in 2014. The Commission President and the other 27 Commissioners are appointed by agreement among the member states, subject to the approval of the European Parliament.

Greece holds the *Presidency of the Council of Ministers* (often termed the "EU Presidency") from January to June 2014; Italy will hold the Presidency from July to December 2014.

Every two-and-a-half years (twice per each five-year parliamentary term) Members of the European Parliament (MEPs) elect the *President of the European Parliament*, currently German MEP Martin Schulz, of the center-left Progressive Alliance of Socialists and Democrats (S&D) parliamentary group. Elected in January 2012, Schulz replaces Polish MEP Jerzy Buzek, of the center-right European People's Party (EPP) group. Traditionally, the two largest parliamentary groups (currently the EPP and S&D) have agreed to split the position of President during each term.

The *High Representative of the Union for Foreign Affairs and Security Policy* is Catherine Ashton of the United Kingdom. Ashton served previously as the European Commissioner for Trade. The High Representative is chosen by agreement among the member states but like the other members of the Commission, must also be approved by the European Parliament.

WHAT IS THE EURO AND THE EUROZONE CRISIS?

Eighteen of the EU's 28 member states belong to the EU's Economic and Monetary Union (EMU); these 18 countries have agreed to closely coordinate their economic and monetary policies and use a common single currency, the euro.[4] The gradual introduction of the euro began in January 1999 when 11 EU member states became the first to adopt it and banks and many businesses began using the euro as a unit of account. Euro notes and coins replaced national currencies in participating states in January 2002. EMU participants also share a common central bank—the European Central Bank (ECB)—and a common monetary policy. However, they do not have a common fiscal policy and member states retain control over decisions about national spending and taxation, subject to certain conditions designed to maintain budgetary discipline. The 18 EMU participants are often collectively referred to as "the Eurozone."

The "Eurozone crisis" began as a sovereign (or public) debt crisis in Greece in 2009-2010. Over the previous decade, the Greek government borrowed heavily from international capital markets to pay for its budget and trade deficits. This left Greece vulnerable to shifts in investor confidence, which decreased considerably in 2009 amid the global financial crisis and revelations that previous Greek governments had been under-reporting the budget deficit. As investors became increasingly nervous that the Greek government's debt was too high, markets began demanding higher interest rates for Greek bonds, which drove up Greece's borrowing costs and further increased its debt levels. By early 2010, Greece risked defaulting on its public debt. Market concerns soon spread to several other Eurozone countries with high, potentially unsustainable levels of public debt, including Ireland, Portugal, Spain, and Italy. The debt problems of these countries have also posed a risk to the European banking system, slowed economic growth, and led to increased unemployment in many Eurozone countries.

European leaders and EU institutions have responded to the crisis and sought to stem its contagion with a variety of policy mechanisms. In order to avoid default, Greece, Ireland, Portugal, and Cyprus have received "bail-out" loans from the EU and the International Monetary Fund (IMF). Such assistance, however, has come with some strings attached, including the imposition of strict austerity measures. Spain (the Eurozone's fourth-largest economy) has enacted significant austerity measures of its own and Eurozone leaders approved a recapitalization plan for Spanish banks. Other key initiatives have included the creation of a permanent EU financial assistance facility (the European Stability Mechanism, or ESM) to provide emergency support to Eurozone countries in financial trouble; an EU decision to create a single bank supervisor for the Eurozone, under which the ESM would be able to inject cash directly into ailing Eurozone banks; and ECB efforts to calm the financial markets by purchasing large portions of European sovereign debt and providing significant infusions of credit into the European banking system.

At present, the Eurozone crisis appears to have abated to some degree, with market confidence relatively positive since late 2012. EU-IMF financial assistance to Ireland ended in December 2013, and the country has returned to the bond markets. EU aid to Spanish banks has also ceased. However, experts assert that the Eurozone remains fragile as many members continue to struggle with weak economic growth and high unemployment. Some analysts suggest that smaller Eurozone countries, such as Slovenia, may require EU financial assistance in the future, and that Greece may need additional EU-IMF "bail-out" loans.

The Eurozone crisis has also had significant political implications, resulting in the fall of some member state governments, and forcing EU leaders to grapple with both the euro's future viability and the desirability of further EU integration. Some view EU efforts to address the crisis as too timid and too slow in part because of political differences among EU member states and between those in and outside of the Eurozone. Key points of tension have arisen over the proper balance between imposing austerity measures versus stimulating growth, and whether and to what extent the Eurozone countries should pursue closer fiscal integration. In January 2012, 25 of the EU's then-27 member states agreed on a new "fiscal compact" aimed at strengthening fiscal discipline within the EU (in part by requiring national budgets to be in balance or in surplus), providing for a more automatic imposition of sanctions should a country breach EU fiscal rules, and improving the coordination of national economic policies; this pact entered into force in January 2013.[5]

WHY AND HOW IS THE EU ENLARGING?

The EU views the enlargement process as an extraordinary opportunity to promote stability and prosperity in Europe. Since 2004, EU membership has grown from 15 to 28 countries, bringing in most states of Central and Eastern Europe. The EU began as the European Coal and Steel Community in 1952 with six members (Belgium, France, Germany, Italy, Luxembourg, and the Netherlands). In 1973, Denmark, Ireland, and the United Kingdom joined what had then become known as the European Community. Greece joined in 1981, followed by Spain and Portugal in 1986. In 1995, Austria, Finland, and Sweden acceded to the present-day European Union. In 2004, the EU welcomed eight former communist countries—the Czech Republic, Estonia, Hungary, Latvia, Lithuania, Poland, Slovakia, and Slovenia—plus Cyprus and Malta as new members. Bulgaria and Romania joined in 2007. Croatia became the 28th member of the EU on July 1, 2013.

In order to be eligible for EU membership, countries must first meet a set of established criteria, including having a functioning democracy and market economy. Once a country becomes an official candidate, accession negotiations are a long and complex process in which the applicant must adopt and implement a massive body of EU laws and regulations. Analysts contend that the carefully managed process of enlargement is one of the EU's most powerful policy tools, and that, over the years, it has helped transform many European countries into functioning democracies and more affluent societies.

Five countries are currently recognized by the EU as official candidates for membership: Macedonia, Montenegro, Serbia, Turkey, and Iceland.[6] All are at different stages of the accession process. The remaining western Balkan states of Albania, Bosnia-Herzegovina, and Kosovo are recognized as potential future EU candidates, but most experts assess that it will likely be many years before any of them are ready to join the EU.

The EU maintains that the enlargement door remains open to any European country that fulfills the EU's political and economic criteria for membership. Nevertheless, some European leaders and many EU citizens are cautious about additional EU expansion, especially to Turkey or countries farther east, such as Georgia or Ukraine, in the longer term. Worries about continued EU enlargement range from fears of unwanted migrant labor to the implications of an ever-expanding Union on the EU's institutions, finances, and overall identity. Observers note that such qualms are particularly apparent with respect to Turkey's possible EU accession, given Turkey's large size, predominantly Muslim culture, and relatively less prosperous economy.[7]

DOES THE EU HAVE A FOREIGN POLICY?

The EU has a Common Foreign and Security Policy (CFSP), in which member states adopt common policies, undertake joint actions, and pursue coordinated strategies in areas in which they can reach consensus. CFSP was established in 1993; the eruption of hostilities in the Balkans in the early 1990s and the EU's limited tools for responding to the crisis convinced EU leaders that the Union had to improve its ability to act collectively in the foreign policy realm. Previous EU attempts to further such political integration had foundered for decades on member state concerns about protecting national sovereignty and different foreign policy prerogatives.

CFSP decision-making is dominated by the member states and requires the unanimous agreement of all 28. Member states must also ensure that national policies are in line with agreed EU strategies and positions (e.g., imposing sanctions on a country). However, CFSP does not preclude individual member states pursuing their own national foreign policies or conducting their own national diplomacy.

CFSP remains a work in progress. Although many view the EU as having made considerable strides in forging common policies on a range of international issues, from the Balkans to the Middle East peace process to Iran, others argue that the credibility of CFSP too often suffers from an inability to reach consensus. The launch of the U.S.-led war in Iraq in 2003, for example, was extremely divisive among EU members, and they were unable to agree on a common EU position. Others note that some differences in viewpoint are inevitable among 28 countries that still retain different approaches, cultures, histories, and relationships—and often different national interests—when it comes to foreign policy.

The EU's Lisbon Treaty seeks to bolster CFSP by increasing the EU's visibility on the world stage and making the EU a more coherent foreign policy actor. As noted above, the treaty establishes a High Representative of the Union for Foreign Affairs and Security Policy to serve essentially as the EU's chief diplomat. This post combines into one position the former responsibilities of the Council of Ministers' High Representative for CFSP and the Commissioner for External Relations, who previously managed the European Commission's diplomatic activities and foreign aid programs. In doing so, the High Representative position seeks to marry the EU's collective political influence with the Commission's economic weight and development tools. The Lisbon Treaty also creates a new EU diplomatic corps (the European External Action Service) to support the High Representative.[8]

DOES THE EU HAVE A DEFENSE POLICY?

Since 1999, the EU has been working to develop a Common Security and Defense Policy (CSDP), formerly known as the European Security and Defense Policy (ESDP).[9] CSDP seeks to improve the EU's ability to respond to crises, enhance European military capabilities, and give the EU's common foreign policy a military backbone. The EU has created three defense decision-making bodies, has set targets for improving defense capabilities, and has developed a rapid reaction force and multinational "battlegroups." Such EU forces are not a standing "EU army," but rather a catalogue of troops and assets at appropriate readiness levels that may be drawn from existing national forces for EU operations.

CSDP operations focus largely on tasks such as peacekeeping, crisis management, and humanitarian assistance. Many CSDP missions to date have been civilian, rather than military, in nature, with objectives such as police and judicial training ("rule of law") or security sector reform. The EU is or has been engaged in CSDP missions in regions ranging from the Balkans and the Caucasus to Africa and the Middle East.

However, improving European military capabilities has been difficult, especially given flat or declining European defense budgets. Serious capability gaps continue to exist in strategic air- and sealift, command and control systems, intelligence, and other force multipliers. Also, a relatively low percentage of European forces are deployable for expeditionary operations. Some analysts have suggested pooling assets among several member states and the development of national niche capabilities as possible ways to help remedy European military shortfalls. In 2004, the EU established the European Defense Agency to help coordinate defense-industrial and procurement policy in an effort to stretch European defense funds farther.

WHAT IS THE RELATIONSHIP OF THE EU TO NATO?

Since its inception, the EU has asserted that CSDP is intended to allow the EU to make decisions and conduct military operations "where NATO as a whole is not engaged," and that CSDP is not aimed at usurping NATO's collective defense role. The United States has supported EU efforts to develop CSDP provided that it remains tied to NATO, does not rival or duplicate NATO structures or resources, and does not weaken the transatlantic alliance. Advocates of CSDP argue that building more robust EU military capabilities will also benefit NATO given that 22 countries belong to both NATO and the EU.[10] The Berlin Plus arrangement—which was finalized in 2003 and allows EU-led military missions access to NATO planning capabilities and common assets— was designed to help ensure close NATO-EU links and prevent a wasteful duplication of European defense resources. Since then, two Berlin Plus missions have been conducted in the Balkans, and NATO and the EU have sought to coordinate their activities on the ground in operations in Afghanistan and various hot spots in Africa.

Nevertheless, NATO-EU relations remain somewhat strained. Closer and more extensive NATOEU cooperation at the political level on a range of issues—from discussions on countering terrorism or weapons proliferation to improving coordination of crisis management planning and defense policies— has been stymied largely by EU tensions with Turkey (in NATO but not the EU) and the ongoing dispute over the divided island of Cyprus (in the EU but not NATO).[11] Many analysts argue that until a political settlement is reached over Cyprus, enhanced NATO-EU cooperation is unlikely. Others suggest that additional reasons exist for frictions in the NATO-EU relationship, including bureaucratic rivalry and competition between the two organizations and varying views on both sides of the Atlantic regarding the future roles and missions of both NATO and the EU's CSDP. Some U.S. officials still worry that a minority of EU member states would like to build an EU defense arm more independent from NATO in the longer term.

WHAT IS JUSTICE AND HOME AFFAIRS (JHA)?

The JHA field seeks to foster common internal security measures while protecting the fundamental rights of EU citizens and promoting the free movement of persons within the EU zone. JHA encompasses police and judicial cooperation, immigration, asylum, border controls, fighting terrorism and other cross-border crimes such as drug trafficking, and combating racism and xenophobia. For many years, however, EU efforts to harmonize policies in the JHA field were hampered by member states' concerns that such measures could infringe on their legal systems and national sovereignty. The 2001 terrorist attacks on the United States, the subsequent revelation of Al Qaeda cells in Europe, and the terrorist bombings in Madrid and London in 2004 and 2005, however, helped give new momentum to many initiatives in the JHA area. Among other measures, the EU has established a common definition of terrorism, an EU-wide arrest warrant, and new tools to strengthen external EU border controls.

The EU's Lisbon Treaty gives the European Parliament "co-decision" power over the majority of JHA policy areas. The Treaty also makes most decisions on JHA issues in the Council of Ministers subject to the qualified majority voting system, rather than unanimity, in a bid to strengthen JHA further and speed EU decision-making. In practice, however, the EU will likely still seek consensus as much as possible on sensitive JHA policies. Moreover, for some issues in the JHA area, the EU has added an "emergency brake" that allows any member state to halt a measure it believes could threaten its national legal system and ultimately, to opt-out of it. Despite these safeguards, the UK and Ireland negotiated the right to choose those JHA policies they want to take part in and to opt out of all others; Denmark extended its previous JHA opt-out in some JHA areas to all JHA issues. The Lisbon Treaty technically renames JHA as the "Area of Freedom, Security, and Justice."

DOES THE EU HAVE A TRADE POLICY AND PROCESS?

The EU has a common external trade policy, which means that trade policy is an exclusive competence of the EU and no member state can negotiate its own international trade agreement. The EU's trade policy is one of its most well-developed and integrated policies. It evolved along with the common market—which provides for the free movement of goods within the EU—to prevent one member state from importing foreign goods at cheaper prices due to lower tariffs and then re-exporting the items to another member with higher tariffs. The scope of the common trade policy has been extended partially to include trade in services, the defense of intellectual property rights, and foreign direct investment. The European Commission and the Council of Ministers work together to set the common customs tariff, guide export policy, and decide on trade protection or retaliation measures where necessary. EU rules allow the Council to make trade decisions with qualified majority voting, but in practice the Council tends to employ consensus.

The European Commission negotiates trade agreements with outside countries and trading blocs on behalf of the Union as a whole. As a result of the Lisbon Treaty, both the Council of Ministers and the European Parliament must approve all such trade agreements before they can enter into force. The process for negotiating and concluding a new international trade agreement begins with discussions among all three EU institutions and a Commission impact assessment, including a public consultation on the content and options for any future trade accord. Provided there is a general agreement to proceed, the Commission initiates an informal scoping exercise with the potential partner country or trade bloc on the range and extent of topics to be considered in the negotiations. Following this dialogue, the Commission then formulates what are known as "negotiating directives" (sometimes termed the "negotiating mandate"), which sets out the Commission's overall objectives for the future agreement. The "directives" are submitted to the Council for its approval, and shared with the European Parliament.

Provided the Council approves the "negotiating directives," the Commission then launches formal negotiations for the new trade agreement on behalf of the EU. Within the Commission, the department that handles EU trade policy—the Directorate General for Trade (DG Trade)—leads the negotiations but draws on expertise from across the Commission. Typically, there are a series of negotiation rounds; the duration of the negotiations varies but can range from two to three years or longer. During the course of negotiations, the Commission is expected to keep both the Council and the

Parliament apprized of its progress and the Council and the Parliament may take the opportunity to voice their respective views and concerns. The Parliament may conduct its own oversight hearings through its International Trade Committee (INTA). When negotiations reach the final stage, both parties to the agreement initial the proposed accord. It is then submitted to the Council and the Parliament for review.[12] If the Council approves the accord, it authorizes the Commission to formally sign the agreement.

Once the new trade accord is officially signed by both parties, the Council submits a draft decision to conclude negotiations to the Parliament for its consent. The Parliament reviews the signed agreement both in the INTA Committee and in plenary session. Although the Parliament is limited to voting "yes" or "no" to the new accord, it can indicate that it would not support the agreement should it find fault with any of its provisions, and can ask the Commission to review or address its concerns. If parts of the trade agreement fall under member state competence, all EU countries must also ratify the agreement according to their national ratification procedures.[13] After Parliament gives its consent and following ratification in the member states (if required), the Council adopts the final decision to conclude the agreement. It may then be officially published and enter into force.[14]

HOW DO EU COUNTRIES AND CITIZENS VIEW THE EU?

EU member states have long believed that the Union magnifies their political and economic clout (i.e., the sum is greater than the parts). Nevertheless, tensions have always existed within the EU between those members that seek an "ever closer union" through greater integration and those that prefer to keep the Union on a more intergovernmental footing in order to better guard their national sovereignty. As a result, some member states over the years have "opted out" of certain aspects of integration, such as passport- and visa-free travel within the EU (UK and Ireland), the euro (UK, Denmark, and Sweden), Justice and Home Affairs issues (UK, Ireland, and Denmark), and the common defense policy (Denmark). Another classic divide in the EU falls along big versus small state lines; small members are often cautious of initiatives that they fear could allow larger countries to dominate EU decision-making. In addition, the EU's enlargement to the east has brought in many new members with histories of Soviet control, which may color their views on issues ranging from EU reform to relations with Russia or the Middle East; at times, such differences have caused frictions with older EU member states.

The prevailing view among European publics has likewise been historically favorable toward the EU. Despite the EU's recent financial troubles and a drop in public support for the EU's single currency, surveys indicate that the majority of EU citizens continue to consider EU membership as good for their countries overall.[15] EU citizens also value the freedom to easily travel, work, and live in other EU countries. At the same time, there has always been a certain amount of "Euroskepticism" among some segments of the European public. Traditionally, such skepticism has been driven by fears about the loss of national sovereignty or concerns about what some view as a "democratic deficit" in the EU—a feeling that ordinary citizens have no say over decisions taken in far-away Brussels. Recently, however, the Eurozone crisis has helped increase the degree of Euro-skepticism in some countries, such as the UK, and along with fears about immigration and globalization, has contributed to the rise of anti-EU populist parties in a number of member states, including Austria, France, Finland, Sweden, and the Netherlands.

DOES THE UNITED STATES HAVE A FORMAL RELATIONSHIP WITH THE EU?

For decades, the United States and the EU (and its progenitors) have maintained diplomatic and economic ties. Despite some frictions, the United States and the EU share a dynamic political partnership on an increasing number of foreign policy issues, and U.S.-EU trade and investment relations are close and extensive. The 1990 U.S.-EU Transatlantic Declaration set out principles for greater consultation, and established regular summit and ministerial meetings. In 1995, the New Transatlantic Agenda (NTA) and the EU-U.S. Joint Action Plan provided a framework for promoting stability and democracy together, responding to global challenges, and expanding world trade. The NTA also sought to strengthen individual, people-to-people ties across the Atlantic, and launched a number of dialogues, including ones for business leaders and legislators. The Transatlantic Legislators' Dialogue (TLD) has been the formal mechanism for engagement and exchange between the U.S. House of Representatives and the European Parliament since 1999, although inter-parliamentary exchanges between the two bodies date back to 1972.

WHO ARE U.S. OFFICIALS' COUNTERPARTS IN THE EU?

U.S.-EU summits usually occur at least once a year; under the Lisbon Treaty, the U.S. President meets with the President of the European Commission and the President of the European Council. The U.S. Secretary of State's most frequent interlocutor in the EU context is the High Representative for the Union's Foreign Affairs and Security Policy. The U.S. Trade Representative's key interlocutor is the European Commissioner for Trade, who directs the EU's common external trade policy. Other U.S. Cabinet-level officials interact with Commission counterparts or member state ministers in the Council of Ministers formation as issues arise. Many working-level relationships between U.S. and EU officials also exist. A delegation in Washington, DC, represents the European Union in its dealings with the U.S. government, while the U.S. Mission to the European Union represents Washington's interests in Brussels.

HOW ARE U.S.-EU POLITICAL RELATIONS DOING?

The United States has supported the European integration project since its inception as a way to foster democratic allies and strong trading partners in Europe. During the Cold War, the EU project was viewed as central to deterring the Soviet threat. Today, the United States often looks to the EU for partnership on an extensive range of common foreign policy challenges—from countering terrorism and weapons proliferation to ensuring the stability of international financial markets—and the two sides have a proven track record of close cooperation on a multitude of global concerns. Over the last decade, for example, the United States and the EU have promoted peace and stability in the Balkans and Afghanistan, worked together to contain Iran's nuclear ambitions, and have significantly strengthened their law enforcement and counterterrorism cooperation. In recent years, U.S. and EU policies have been largely aligned in response to the changes in the Middle East and North Africa resulting from the "Arab Spring," and the United States and the EU have sought to exert diplomatic pressure and impose sanctions on Syria in an effort to end that country's bloody civil war.

At times, however, the U.S.-EU political relationship has faced serious challenges. U.S.-EU relations hit a historic low in 2003 over the U.S.-led invasion of Iraq, which some EU members supported and others strongly opposed. In the aftermath of that crisis, the former George W. Bush Administration sought to improve cooperation and emphasize areas of partnership with the EU. U.S.-EU tensions on several key issues, such as Iran and the Israeli-Palestinian conflict, began to dissipate. The Obama Administration has also worked to bolster ties with the EU and has expanded cooperation on other issues, such as cybersecurity and energy security.

Nevertheless, U.S.-EU differences persist in other areas. Data privacy has been and continues to be a key U.S.-EU sticking point. Some European officials, including many Members of the European Parliament (MEPs), have long worried that several U.S.-EU law enforcement and counterterrorism information-sharing arrangements do not sufficiently protect European citizens' data privacy rights. European concerns have been heightened since the June 2013 revelations of U.S. National Security Agency surveillance programs, press reports suggesting that U.S. intelligence agencies have monitored EU diplomatic offices, and subsequent allegations of other U.S. intelligence operations in Europe (including reported phone record collection efforts in France and Spain as well as the past monitoring of German Chancellor Angela Merkel's mobile phone). In response, some MEPs are now demanding stronger safeguards for personal data transferred outside of the EU, and many experts contend that the purported U.S. surveillance activities will likely make concluding future U.S.-EU information-sharing agreements more difficult. Analysts also worry that such alleged U.S. activities could foster mistrust between the two sides and negatively affect the broader U.S.-EU relationship, including the prospects for a comprehensive Transatlantic Trade and Investment Partnership (see below).[16]

In addition, some European leaders have recently expressed concerns about the U.S. "pivot" or rebalancing toward Asia. U.S. officials stress that this rebalancing will not come at the expense of the transatlantic relationship and that the United States hopes to engage more closely with Europe in the future on issues of economic and strategic importance in Asia. Meanwhile, some U.S. policymakers continue to worry that the Eurozone crisis could lead to a more inward-focused EU, preoccupied with its own economic and political problems, and less able to be a robust partner for the United States in tackling common international challenges.

HOW ARE U.S.-EU ECONOMIC RELATIONS DOING?

The United States and the EU share the largest trade and investment relationship in the world. Despite the 2008-2009 global economic downturn, the combined U.S. and EU economies account for over 50% of global gross domestic product, roughly 25% of global exports, and 31% of global imports. According to one recent study, the transatlantic economy generates over $5 trillion in commercial sales a year and employs up to 15 million workers on both sides of the Atlantic. Of particular importance is the fact that U.S. and European companies are the biggest investors in each other's economies (total stock of two-way direct investment was almost $3.7 trillion as of 2011) and the United States and Europe remain each other's most profitable markets.[17]

Although the vast majority of the U.S.-EU economic relationship is harmonious, some tensions exist. U.S.-EU trade disputes persist over poultry, bio-engineered food products, protection of geographical indications, and subsidies to Boeing and Airbus. Many analysts note that resolving U.S.-EU trade disputes has become increasingly difficult, in part because both sides are of roughly equal economic strength and neither has the ability to impose concessions on the other. Another factor may be that many disputes involve differences in domestic values, political priorities, and regulatory frameworks. The United States and the EU have made a number of attempts to reduce remaining non-tariff and regulatory barriers to trade and investment. The Transatlantic Economic Council (TEC) was created at the 2007 U.S.-EU summit and tasked with advancing the process of regulatory cooperation and trade barrier reduction.

Over the last few years, the global economic downturn and the Eurozone crisis have also challenged the U.S.-EU relationship. Given the extensive transatlantic economic ties, U.S. officials worried that the EU's debt crisis could adversely affect U.S. exports to and sales of U.S. companies in Europe, or that ripple effects could weaken U.S. financial institutions and push the United States back into recession should any Eurozone member default. In response, the Obama Administration urged the EU to take forceful action to address the debt crisis and advocated for more substantial financial assistance for struggling Eurozone economies. Although U.S. concerns about the Eurozone crisis have diminished amid U.S. economic growth and increasing market stability in Europe, some U.S. policymakers continue to question what they view as the EU's emphasis on austerity measures, believing that greater efforts are needed to promote growth.

In light of the fiscal and economic difficulties on both sides of the Atlantic, in November 2011, U.S. and EU leaders directed the TEC to establish a High Level Working Group (HLWG) on Jobs and Growth. The HLWG was charged with considering ways to increase U.S.-EU trade and investment to stimulate more job creation and economic growth on both sides of the Atlantic.

Based on the recommendations in the HLWG's final report, the United States and the EU launched negotiations in July 2013 on an ambitious, high-standard free trade agreement, known as the Transatlantic Trade and Investment Partnership (TTIP). Both sides hope that the TTIP negotiations will result in an agreement that further opens markets and increases U.S. and EU exports; strengthens rules-based investment; tackles costly non-tariff barriers; reduces regulatory barriers; and enhances cooperation on trade issues of global concern.[18]

Historically, U.S.-EU cooperation has been a driving force behind efforts to liberalize world trade and ensure the stability of international financial markets. U.S. and EU leaders have sought to pursue a coordinated response to the global financial crisis through the G-20, which brings together industrialized and developing countries. And many view U.S.-EU cooperation as crucial to managing emerging economies such as China, India, and Brazil in the years ahead. At the same time, divisions exist both among EU countries and between the EU and the United States in some policy areas. U.S.-EU disagreement over agricultural subsidies, for example, has contributed to the stalemated Doha Round of multilateral trade negotiations. U.S.-European differences also persist about how to curb large global trade imbalances viewed as posing serious risks to economic growth and an open international trading system.

End Notes

[1] The 28 members of the EU are: Austria, Belgium, Bulgaria, Croatia, Cyprus, the Czech Republic, Denmark, Estonia, Finland, France, Germany, Greece, Hungary, Ireland, Italy, Latvia, Lithuania, Luxembourg, Malta, the Netherlands, Poland, Portugal, Romania, Slovakia, Slovenia, Spain, Sweden, and the United Kingdom.

[2] The Lisbon Treaty amends, rather than replaces, existing EU treaties. The history of the Lisbon Treaty is replete with contentious negotiations among the member states and numerous ratification hurdles; it evolved from the proposed EU constitutional treaty, which was rejected in French and Dutch national referendums in 2005. Despite the failure of the EU constitutional treaty, experts say the Lisbon Treaty preserves over 90% of the substance of

The European Union: Questions and Answers

the original treaty. For more information, see CRS Report RS21618, The European Union's Reform Process: The Lisbon Treaty, by Kristin Archick and Derek E. Mix.

[3] The Lisbon Treaty technically renames the "co-decision" procedure as the "ordinary legislative procedure."

[4] The 18 members of the EU that use the euro are: Austria, Belgium, Cyprus, Estonia, Finland, France, Germany, Greece, Ireland, Italy, Latvia, Luxembourg, Malta, the Netherlands, Portugal, Slovakia, Slovenia, and Spain.

[5] For more information, see CRS Report R42377, The Eurozone Crisis: Overview and Issues for Congress, coordinated by Rebecca M. Nelson.

[6] Although the EU continues to recognize Iceland as an official candidate for membership, Iceland's accession negotiations have been on hold since May 2013, when a new Icelandic coalition government largely opposed to EU membership took office.

[7] For more information, see CRS Report RS21344, European Union Enlargement, by Kristin Archick, and CRS Report RS22517, European Union Enlargement: A Status Report on Turkey's Accession Negotiations, by Vincent L. Morelli.

[8] For more information, see CRS Report R41959, The European Union: Foreign and Security Policy, by Derek E. Mix.

[9] ESDP was renamed CSDP by the Lisbon Treaty.

[10] Six countries belong to the EU, but not to NATO (Austria, Cyprus, Finland, Ireland, Malta, and Sweden); six other ones currently belong to NATO but not the EU (Albania, Canada, Iceland, Norway, Turkey, and the United States).

[11] Turkey continues to formally object to Cypriot participation in NATO-EU meetings on the grounds that Cyprus is not a member of NATO's Partnership for Peace (PfP) and thus does not have a security relationship with the alliance. The absence of Cyprus from PfP also hinders NATO and the EU from sharing sensitive intelligence information. In the current political climate, Cyprus essentially cannot join PfP because it would require the consent of all NATO allies, including Turkey.

[12] Some trade agreements submitted for Council and Parliament approval are accompanied by Commission legislative proposals needed to implement the new accord; these legislative proposals must also be adopted by both the Council and the Parliament.

[13] With the entrance into force of the Lisbon Treaty, most policy areas usually included in trade agreements are now considered areas of exclusive EU competence; thus, most experts judge that member state ratification may be unnecessary, or required only for small parts of new EU trade agreements. See Stephen Woolcock, "EU Trade and Investment Policymaking After the Lisbon Treaty," Intereconomics, 2010.

[14] For more on the EU process for concluding new trade agreements, see European Commission, "Factsheet: Trade Negotiations Step By Step," June 2012, http://trade.ec.europa.eu/doculib/docs/2012/june/tradoc_149616.pdf.

[15] See for example, the German Marshall Fund of the United States, Transatlantic Trends 2013.

[16] James Fontanella-Khan, "MEPs Call for Clause to Limit American Internet Snooping," Financial Times, June 19, 2013; Michael Birnbaum, "EU Fury on Allegations of U.S. Spying," Washington Post, June 30, 2013; Alison Smale, "Indignation Over U.S. Spying Spreads in Europe," New York Times, October 24, 2013.

[17] Daniel S. Hamilton and Joseph P. Quinlan, The Transatlantic Economy 2013: Annual Survey of Jobs, Trade, and Investment between the United States and Europe, Center for Transatlantic Relations, 2013. Also see CRS Report RL30608, EU-U.S. Economic Ties: Framework, Scope, and Magnitude, by William H. Cooper.

[18] Office of the United States Trade Representative, "Fact Sheet: United States To Negotiate Transatlantic Trade and Investment Partnership with the European Union," February 13, 2013. Also see CRS Report R43158, Proposed Transatlantic Trade and Investment Partnership (TTIP): In Brief, by Shayerah Ilias Akhtar and Vivian C. Jones.

In: Democratic Credentials of the European Union   ISBN: 978-1-63321-628-0
Editor: Evonne Graham   © 2014 Nova Science Publishers, Inc.

Chapter 2

THE EUROPEAN PARLIAMENT[*]

Kristin Archick

SUMMARY

Between May 22 and May 25, 2014, the 28 member states of the European Union (EU) held elections for the next European Parliament (EP). The Parliament is a key EU institution that represents the citizens of the EU. It works closely with the two other main EU bodies, the European Commission (the EU's executive) and the Council of the European Union (also known as the Council of Ministers, on which the national governments of the EU's 28 member states are represented). Members of the European Parliament (MEPs) serve five-year terms, and have been directly elected since 1979. The next EP will have 751 seats.

Once limited to being a consultative assembly, the EP has accumulated more power over time. Experts assert that the EU's latest effort at institutional reform—the Lisbon Treaty, which entered into force on December 1, 2009—has increased the relative power of the EP within the EU considerably. The EP now shares legislative power with the Council of Ministers in most policy areas, giving the EP the right to accept, amend, or reject the vast majority of EU laws (with some exceptions in areas such as tax matters or foreign policy). The Lisbon Treaty also gives the EP the power to decide on the allocation of the EU budget jointly with the Council, the right to approve or reject international agreements, and greater decision-making authority on trade-

---

[*] This is an edited, reformatted and augmented version of a Congressional Research Service publication, No. RS21998, dated May 19, 2014.

related issues. At the same time, some analysts contend that the EP still lacks the legitimacy of national parliaments and that many European citizens remain unaware of the EP's role within the EU.

Members of the European Parliament (MEPs) are organized into political groups, which caucus according to political ideology rather than nationality. The EP's standing committees are key actors in the adoption of EU legislation, and EP delegations maintain international parliament-toparliament relations. In the upcoming EP elections, anti-EU or "euroskeptic" political parties— which are predominantly nationalistic, populist, and on the far right of the political spectrum, although a few are on the left or far left—appear poised to make moderate to significant gains in several EU countries. As a result, some analysts suggest that they could alter the political composition of the next EP and have implications for the EU's legislative and policymaking processes over the next five years, especially if hardline elements are able to form a new political group. Other experts question the ability of these euroskeptic parties to forge a united front in a way that would significantly affect the functioning and character of the next EP.

The EP has not been shy about exerting its new powers under the Lisbon Treaty, and in some areas, with implications for U.S. interests. For example, EP concerns about U.S. data privacy safeguards have complicated U.S.-EU negotiations in the past on several information-sharing agreements aimed at countering terrorism. Following the initial unauthorized disclosures in June 2013 of U.S. National Security Agency surveillance programs and subsequent allegations that U.S. intelligence agencies have monitored EU diplomatic offices and engaged in other surveillance activities in Europe, many analysts worry about whether future U.S.-EU information-sharing agreements will be able to secure the necessary EP approval. In addition, EP approval will ultimately be required to allow any eventual U.S.-EU agreement on a Transatlantic Trade and Investment Partnership (TTIP) to enter into force.

Ties between the EP and the U.S. Congress are long-standing, and institutional cooperation currently exists through the Transatlantic Legislators' Dialogue (TLD). In light of the EP's growing role as an actor in the conduct of U.S.-EU relations, the EP and its activities may be of increasing interest to the 113th Congress.

THE EUROPEAN PARLIAMENT: A KEY EU INSTITUTION

The European Parliament (EP) is a key institution of the European Union (EU). The EU is a political and economic partnership that represents a unique form of cooperation among its 28 member states.[1] The EU is the latest stage of

The European Parliament

a process of European integration begun in the 1950s to promote peace and economic prosperity in Europe; the EU has been built through a series of binding treaties, and its members have committed to harmonizing laws and adopting common policies on an extensive range of issues. EU member states work together through common institutions to set policy and promote their collective interests.

As the only EU institution that is directly elected, the European Parliament represents the citizens of the EU. Once limited to being a consultative assembly, the EP has accumulated more power over time. Successive EU treaties have enhanced the EP's role and responsibilities in an attempt to improve democratic accountability in the EU policymaking process.

Experts assert that the EU's most recent treaty, the Lisbon Treaty—which took effect on December 1, 2009—has increased the relative power of the EP within the EU significantly. The Lisbon Treaty contains a wide range of internal reforms aimed at improving the effectiveness of the EU's governing institutions, increasing democratic transparency within the EU, and giving the EU a more coherent voice and identity on the world stage. Among other measures, the Lisbon Treaty strengthens the EP's role in the EU's legislative and budgeting processes, gives the EP the right to approve or reject international agreements, and bolsters the EP's decision-making authority on trade-related issues. Many Members of the European Parliament (MEPs) view the EP as one of the big "winners" of this latest round of EU institutional reform.

The EP also works closely with the two other main EU institutions—the European Commission and the Council of the European Union (also known as the Council of Ministers). Despite the EP's growing power and influence, the EP is not widely considered a legislative body in the traditional sense because it cannot initiate legislation; that right rests largely with the Commission, which functions as the EU's executive. However, the EP shares the power to adopt most EU legislation jointly with the Council, composed of ministers of the 28 member states. Some analysts contend that the EP has a limited power of legislative initiative in that the EP can ask the Commission to introduce a legislative proposal, but others note that the Commission is not required to comply with the EP's request.

Between May 22 and May 25, 2014, the 28 member states of the EU held elections for the next EP. The incoming EP will have 751 seats (down from the current Parliament's 766 seat count as a result of changes introduced by the Lisbon Treaty). Some analysts suggest that the recent rise of anti-EU or "euroskeptic" political parties in several EU member states may have significant implications for the upcoming EP elections and the composition of the next EP.

Other EU Institutions

The *European Council* brings together the Heads of State or Government of the member states and the President of the European Commission at least four times a year (in what are often termed "EU Summits"). It acts principally as a strategic guide and driving force for EU policy. The European Council is headed by a President, who serves as the coordinator and spokesman for the work of the 28 Heads of State or Government.

The *European Commission* upholds the common interest of the Union as a whole. It is independent of the member states' national governments. As the EU's executive, the Commission has the sole right of legislative initiative in most cases and implements EU decisions and common policies. It also serves as the guardian of the EU's treaties, ensuring that member states adopt and abide by their provisions. The 28 Commissioners, one from each EU country, are appointed by agreement among the member states to five-year terms. One Commissioner serves as Commission President. Each of the other Commissioners holds a distinct portfolio (e.g., agriculture, energy, trade), similar to U.S. department secretaries and agency directors.

The *Council of the European Union (Council of Ministers)* represents the national governments of the 28 member states. The Council enacts legislation based on proposals put forward by the Commission and agreed to (in most cases) by the Parliament; in some sensitive areas such as taxation and foreign policy, however, the Council retains decision-making authority. A minister from each country takes part in Council meetings, with participation configured according to the subject under consideration (e.g., agriculture ministers would meet to discuss farm subsidies). The Presidency of the Council rotates among the member states, changing every six months.

The *Court of Justice* interprets EU law, and its rulings are binding. The *Court of Auditors* monitors the Union's financial management. A number of other *advisory committees* represent economic, social, and regional interests.

ROLE OF THE EUROPEAN PARLIAMENT

Legislative Process

The role of the European Parliament in the legislative process has expanded steadily over time as the scope of EU policy has grown. Initially, the EP was limited to offering nonbinding opinions in a "consultation procedure." The EP began to gain more power to affect EU legislation in the "cooperation procedure" of the 1986 Single European Act.

The introduction of the "co-decision procedure" in the Maastricht Treaty of 1992, however, significantly enhanced the EP's role in the EU's legislative process in some areas, especially those related to the EU's common internal market. In the "co-decision procedure," the EP and the Council of Ministers share legislative power and must both approve a Commission proposal for it to become EU law; through "co-decision," the EP has the right to accept, amend, or reject proposed EU legislation. The Amsterdam Treaty of 1997 extended the use of "co-decision" to many additional policy areas (ranging from the environment to social policy). As more decisions within the Council of Ministers have become subject to a complex majority voting system rather than unanimity to allow for greater speed and efficiency of decision-making, the Parliament's right of "co-decision" has come to be viewed as an increasingly important democratic counterweight at the European level to the Commission and Council.

As noted above, the Lisbon Treaty strengthens the EP's responsibilities, especially in the EU's legislative process. It roughly doubles the Parliament's right of "co-decision" to almost 80 policy areas, including agriculture and justice and home affairs issues such as immigration and police cooperation. In doing so, the Lisbon Treaty gives the EP a say—equal to that of the member states in the Council of Ministers—over the vast majority of legislation passed in the EU. Tax matters, social security, and most aspects of foreign policy, however, are among the areas in which EU member states retain decision-making authority and to which the "co-decision procedure" does not apply. The Lisbon Treaty technically renames the "co-decision procedure" as the "ordinary legislative procedure," although the term "co-decision" continues to be used frequently in practice.

Additionally, in the "consent procedure," the EP must, by a simple "yes" or "no" majority, approve the accession of new EU member states and the conclusion of agreements with third parties, such as association and trade agreements with nonmember states.[2] If the Parliament does not give its consent, such agreements cannot enter into force. The EP may also issue nonbinding resolutions, subject to a simple majority.

The "Co-decision Procedure"

The EU's "ordinary legislative procedure," or "co-decision," can be summarized as follows:

(1) if Parliament and the Council of Ministers agree on a Commission proposal, it is approved;

(2) if they disagree, the Council forms a common position; the EP can then either accept the Council's common position, or reject or amend it, by an absolute majority of its members;

(3) if the Council cannot accept the EP's amendments, a conciliation meeting is convened, after which the EP and the Council approve an agreement if one can be reached. If they are unable to agree, the proposal is not adopted.

Budgetary Process

The EP and the Council of Ministers together constitute the EU's budget authority and are responsible for allocating the EU's annual budget; they decide, for example, on the amount of funding dedicated to infrastructure as opposed to education. However, neither the EP nor the Council can affect the size of the EU's annual budget; that amount is fixed periodically by agreement among the EU's member states as a percentage of the Union's combined gross national income (GNI).[3] The EU's 2014 budget is EUR 143 billion (roughly $195 billion) in commitments and EUR 136 billion (or $186 billion) in payments.[4]

With the entrance into force of the Lisbon Treaty, the Parliament has the right to decide on the allocation of the entire EU budget jointly with the Council. Previously, the EP had the last word on "noncompulsory" expenditures, such as development aid, but the Council had the final say on "compulsory" expenditures, such as spending related to agriculture or international agreements. The Lisbon Treaty eliminates the distinction between "compulsory" and "noncompulsory" expenditures. Of particular importance, the EP gains more control over agricultural spending, which usually accounts for over one-third of the EU's annual budget.

Under the Lisbon Treaty, the EU's annual budgetary procedure begins with the Commission proposing a draft budget. The Council adopts its position on the draft budget, including any amendments, and sends it to the EP for its consideration. The Parliament then has 42 days to either approve the draft budget or amend it and send it back to the Council. If the Council agrees with the EP's amendments, the budget is adopted; if the Council disagrees with the EP's changes, a Conciliation Committee is convened to resolve differences and reach agreement on a joint text within 21 days. The joint text must then be approved by both the Council and the EP; however, if the joint text is rejected by the Council, the EP—subject to certain conditions—ultimately has the right to approve the budget. In the event that both the EP and the Council reject the joint text or fail to decide, the Commission must submit a new draft budget. Some EP advocates assert that the EP's position in the annual budgetary process is now stronger than that of the Council, as the Council may never impose a budget against the will of the EP, but under some circumstances, the EP may impose a budget against the will of the Council; at the same time, most experts agree that in practice, the EP would likely only exert this right in exceptional situations.[5]

In determining the EU's annual budget, the EP and the Council must also adhere to annual spending limits laid out in the EU's multi-annual financial framework, which defines the longterm political priorities for the EU and sets annual maximum amounts for each priority and expenditure category.[6] According to the Lisbon Treaty, the Council must agree unanimously on each multiannual financial framework, after having obtained the Parliament's consent.

As such, the Parliament has a degree of input into the EU's overall budgetary direction and the ability to help shape the EU budget to reflect its own political priorities.

In addition, the EP examines the European Commission's implementation of previous annual budgets through the "discharge procedure." In order to close the budget books of a given year, the EP must vote to grant "discharge" based on reports of the EU Court of Auditors and a recommendation of the Council. With its decision, the EP also presents the Commission with binding recommendations and observations regarding implementation of the budget. The EP's budgetary powers are considerably greater than those exercised by most parliaments in EU member states.

Supervision and Oversight Responsibilities

The Parliament has a supervisory role over the European Commission and exercises some limited oversight over the activities of the Council of Ministers. The EP monitors the management of EU policies, can conduct investigations and public hearings, and may submit oral and written questions to the Commission and the Council. The Presidency of the Council, which rotates among the member states every six months, presents its program to the Parliament at the beginning of its term and reports on results achieved at the end of its mandate.

Of particular note, the EP plays a role in the approval process of each new Commission and Commission President every five years. According to the Lisbon Treaty, the member states agree together (usually during a meeting of the European Council) by unanimous consent on who to designate as the Commission President, and their selection must take into account the results of the most recent EP elections. Thus, the relative strengths of the political groups in the EP can affect who is nominated by the member states to this post. For the first time, five of the EP's main political groups have nominated candidates for the next Commission President ahead of the upcoming EP elections in May 2014. Many hope that this will help to improve voter turnout by establishing a "concrete and visible" link between voting in the elections and having a say in determining the future President of the European Commission, thereby also enhancing the EU's democratic legitimacy.

Once a nominee is chosen by the member states to be the next Commission President, he or she then must be "elected" by a majority vote in the EP. Some analysts note that this "election" procedure is also largely intended to raise public awareness of the importance of EP elections and the EP's role in choosing the Commission President; in practice, they assert, it differs very little from the previous parliamentary "approval" process. For example, in both 2004 and 2009—that is, before the Lisbon Treaty's entrance into force—the EP's strongest political group successfully demanded that the Commission President be of the same political stripe. At the same time, given that no single political group in the EP has ever held a majority on its own, the support of other political groups has always been needed in order to approve the nomination. In September 2009, the EP supported the re-appointment of 2004-2009 Commission President José Manuel Barroso for the 2009-2014 term (by a vote of 382 to 219, with 117 abstentions).[7]

Beyond its role in approving the Commission President, the EP also has the power to accept or reject a newly proposed Commission as a whole, but

The European Parliament

not individual nominees. The next European Commission is scheduled to take office on November 1, 2014. Since 1995, the EP has held U.S. Senate-style confirmation hearings for newly designated Commissioners, who are nominated by the member states. In February 2010, the EP voted to approve the so-called Barroso II Commission for the term ending in 2014. Although a new Commission was supposed to have been in place by November 2009, it was held up because of delays in the ratification of the Lisbon Treaty by some member states. The confirmation process for the new Commission was further slowed when the initial Bulgarian nominee withdrew her candidacy in mid-January 2010 after a contentious hearing before the Parliament amid concerns about her past financial dealings and her competence for her portfolio. A similar situation occurred in 2004, when the EP essentially forced the original Italian nominee to the Commission to withdraw due to concerns about his views on homosexuality and women's rights. Some observers view these episodes as signs of the EP's growing confidence and institutional clout.

In addition, the EP may dismiss the entire Commission (although, again, not individual Commissioners) through a vote of censure. To date, the EP has never adopted a motion of censure. However, in 1999, the entire Commission opted to resign rather than face a formal censure by the EP over alleged corruption charges.

ORGANIZATION OF THE EUROPEAN PARLIAMENT

EP Elections

Members of the European Parliament serve five-year terms, and have been directly elected since 1979.[8] Voting for the EP takes place on a national basis, with the number of MEPs elected in each country based roughly on population size. Germany, for example, has the largest number of MEPs (99 in the current Parliament), while Cyprus, Estonia, Luxembourg, and Malta have the fewest (with 6 each).

The last EP elections were held on June 4-7, 2009. Roughly 375 million European citizens were eligible to cast a ballot in 2009. In EP elections, EU citizens may vote or run for a seat in their country of residence, without necessarily holding citizenship in that country. Turnout has declined in every EP election, from an average of 63% in 1979 to a new low of 43% in 2009. (Voter turnout varies greatly from one EU member state to another, however, from around 90% in EU countries where it is mandatory to 20% or lower in others.) Although the average percentage is comparable to turnout in U.S. mid-term elections, some analysts contend that relatively low voter participation compared to European national elections indicates a lack of awareness and understanding about the EP.

As noted previously, EP elections were held May 22-25, 2014, with 751 seats at stake. Many observers suggest that the recent rise of anti-EU or "euroskeptic" political parties in several EU member states may have significant implications for the upcoming EP elections and the composition of the next Parliament. Most of these parties are nationalistic, populist, and far right in political orientation—although a few are on the left or far left— and have been gaining traction in several EU countries, including Austria, Denmark, Finland, France, Greece, Hungary, Italy, the Netherlands, Sweden, and the United Kingdom. Their ascendancy has been fueled by a combination of factors, including Europe's financial crisis and economic downturn; fears about immigration, globalization, and lost national identities; and concerns in some member states about the continued relinquishing of national sovereignty to the EU. Although there is a wide range of euroskeptic parties—from those that advocate an end to the EU and/or the Eurozone to others that seek to reform the Union into a looser entity in which member states would retain greater sovereignty—some analysts estimate that euroskeptic parties combined could make up to 20% of the next EP.[9]

Political Groups

Once elected, Members of the European Parliament caucus according to transnational groups based on political ideology, rather than by nationality. A political group must consist of at least 25 MEPs from a minimum of seven EU member states. The current EP currently has seven political groups—containing over 100 individual political parties—plus a number of "nonattached" or independent members.

Membership in a political group gives MEPs more influence, as groups receive funding from the EP and more speaking time than do nonattached members. The relative size of the political groups helps to determine EP leadership positions and committee posts. The chair or cochairs of each political group also has voting rights in the Conference of Presidents, the political body in Parliament that manages the EP's internal organization. Prior to EP legislative votes, MEPs within each group study the legislative proposals in question with the support of committee reports, discuss prospective

The European Parliament 33

amendments, and seek to arrive at a consensus group position. However, individual MEPs are not bound to vote according to their group's position.

Table 1. Political Groups and Seats in the European Parliament: Results of the 2009 Election and Current Seat Allocations (adjustments reflect the addition of new MEPs in 2011 and 2013)

	2009 Election Results	Current Seat Allocations
European People's Party [Christian Democrats] (EPP; center-right)	265	274
Progressive Alliance of Socialists and Democrats in the European Parliament (S&D; center-left/socialists)	184	196
Alliance of Liberals and Democrats for Europe (ALDE; centrist/liberals)	84	83
Greens/European Free Alliance (Greens-EFA; greens and regionalists)	55	57
European Conservatives and Reformists (ECR; right-wing, anti-federalist)	54	57
European United Left/Nordic Green Left (GUE-NGL; far-left and former communists)	35	35
Europe of Freedom and Democracy (EFD; far-right/euroskeptics)	32	31
Nonattached members	27	33
Total # of Seats in the EP	**736**	**766**

Sources: http://www.europarl.europa.eu/parliament/archive/elections2009/en /index _en.html; http://www.europarl.europa.eu/meps/eu/search.html.

As no single group has ever held an absolute majority in the European Parliament, compromise and coalition-building are important elements of the legislative process. Some analysts assert that distinct ideological definitions between groups are becoming more complicated, as voting blocs form increasingly according to specific issues and interests. Nevertheless, the two largest groups have tended to dominate the Parliament historically.

In the 2009 elections, the *Group of the European People's Party [Christian Democrats] (EPP)* retained its position as the largest political group in the EP. The EPP is center-right in political orientation. In relative terms, the strength of the EPP in the 2009 elections increased significantly due to a sizeable drop in support for center-left parties. Although circumstances and issues differed in each EU member state, some analysts interpreted these results as indicating greater public preference for the approaches of conservative and center-right parties in handling the global financial crisis and recession. However, the center-left *Group of the Progressive Alliance of Socialists and Democrats in the European Parliament (S&D)* remained the EP's second-largest political group following the 2009 elections.

The EPP and the S&D have a history of cross-ideological legislative partnership. As in the 2004- 2009 EP (in which the S&D was called the PES—the Socialist Group in the European Parliament), the two parties have continued to cooperate closely in an unofficial "grand coalition" and together frequently shape politics in the EP. Critics argue that the consensus-seeking of the "grand coalition" makes politics in the EP stale and paradoxical. Other observers note that maximizing consensus and unity lends the EP greater institutional weight. As a general rule, most MEPs prefer consensus outcomes that are endorsed by a large and broad majority.

The third-largest group in the current EP is the *Group of the Alliance of Liberals and Democrats for Europe (ALDE)*. ALDE is centrist and liberal in political orientation (in European political terminology, "liberal" connotes an emphasis on free market economics, individual rights, social equality, and de-centralized government). In the past, ALDE was viewed as the "kingmaker," able to exercise a decisive swing vote for a majority in the EP. However, as a result of some losses suffered by ALDE in the 2009 elections and the shift of the political balance in the EP largely to the right, some analysts assert that ALDE's political capital has decreased. Other observers contend that as the third-largest group, ALDE's position on a given issue has still been a crucial factor in the outcome of many EP votes.

The remaining four political groups in the current EP are smaller in size. On the left side of the political spectrum are the *Group of the Greens/European Free Alliance (Greens-EFA)*; and the *Confederal Group of the European United Left/Nordic Green Left (GUE-NGL)*. The Greens-EFA is largely comprised of numerous European Green parties—leftist in political orientation with a strong emphasis on pro-environment politics and human rights—and several regional parties (e.g., Scottish, Welsh, Basque, and Catalonian) with a leftist or center-left outlook. Despite the overall trend in the EP to the right in the 2009 elections, the Greens-EFA attracted many voters who sought change, resulting in a significant increase in the number of their seats. The GUENGL consists of parties that are even farther left in orientation; some have a Green emphasis while others have roots in communism. The GUE-NGL is pro-EU and pro-integration, but strongly critical of existing EU structures, policies, and overall direction.

The European Parliament 35

On the right side of the political spectrum are two groups formed following the 2009 election: the *European Conservatives and Reformists Group (ECR)*; and the *Europe of Freedom and Democracy Group (EFD)*. The ECR came into existence after the UK Conservative Party broke with the EPP amid growing unease with the EPP's support for continued EU integration. The ECR is right-wing in political orientation, concerned about the loss of national sovereignty in the EU, and opposed to a federal Europe. Even farther to the right is the EFD, composed of euroskeptics and critics of the EU who strongly oppose further European integration.

Many of the "nonattached" or independent members in the current EP hail from far-right extremist parties, which made gains in the 2009 EP elections in a number of countries, such as Austria, Hungary, and the Netherlands. However, these far-right MEPs hold a relatively small number of seats in the current Parliament and appear to have little cohesion among themselves. Analysts note that they have been unable to form a political group and, as a result, their impact in the current EP has been minimal.[10]

Composition of Political Groups in the Current European Parliament

European People's Party (EPP). The center-right EPP contains MEPs from Germany's Christian Democratic/Christian Social Union (CDU-CSU), France's Union pour un Mouvement Populaire (UMP), Spain's Partido Popular (PP), Italy's People of Freedom, Poland's Civic Platform, and numerous other Christian Democratic, conservative, center-right, and centrist national parties. The chair of the EPP is French MEP Joseph Daul.

Progressive Alliance of Socialists and Democrats in the European Parliament (S&D). The center-left S&D includes MEPs from Germany's Social Democratic Party (SPD), France's Socialist Party, the UK Labour Party, Spain's Socialist Party, and numerous other Socialist, Social Democratic, and center-left parties. The chair of S&D is Austrian MEP Hannes Swoboda.

Alliance of Liberals and Democrats for Europe (ALDE). MEPs in the centrist ALDE hail from the UK Liberal Democrats Party, Germany's Free Democrat Party (FDP), and Ireland's Fianna Fail. The chair of ALDE is Belgian MEP (and former Belgian Prime Minister) Guy Verhofstadt.

Greens/European Free Alliance (Greens-EFA). The leftist and pro-environment Greens-EFA includes MEPs from Germany's Alliance '90/The Greens, France's Europe Ecologie, and the Scottish National Party.

The cochairs of the Greens-EFA are French MEP Daniel Cohn-Bendit and German MEP Rebecca Harms.

European Conservatives and Reformists (ECR). The right-wing ECR includes MEPs from the UK Conservative Party, Poland's Law and Justice Party, and the Czech Republic's Civic Democratic Party. The chair of ECR is UK MEP Martin Callanan.

European United Left/Nordic Green Left (GUE-NGL). The far-left GUE-NGL contains MEPs from Germany's Die Linke, the French Communist Party, the Portuguese Communist Party, and the all-Ireland party Sinn Fein. The chair of GUE-NGL is German MEP Gabriele Zimmer.

Europe of Freedom and Democracy (EFD). The largest contingents in the euroskeptic EFD are from the UK Independence Party (UKIP), which advocates UK withdrawal from the EU, and Italy's Lega Nord. The cochairs of EFD are British MEP Nigel Farage and Italian MEP Francesco Enrico Speroni.

Note: This box is meant for illustrative purposes; it is not a definitive or exhaustive list of all the political parties comprising each political group in the European Parliament.

As discussed earlier, a wide spectrum of euroskeptic parties appear poised to make moderate to significant gains in the upcoming EP elections, with more extreme or "hardline" euroskeptics likely to win between 40 to 50 seats. EU officials and mainstream MEPs have expressed concerns that the formation of a far-right, hardline euroskeptic political group could help block legislative initiatives, create gridlock, and hamper efforts toward further EU integration, especially if such a group worked closely with the ECR and the EFD. However, many analysts doubt that the hardliners will be able to meet the EP's numerical and, especially, its geographic requirements for establishing a political group. Those of this view contend that such parties are extremely disparate, with competing nationalist agendas and personalities, as well as a diverse range of social and economic positions based on different traditions and local politics. Moreover, some far-right euroskeptic parties that do not have roots in fascism have been keen to distance themselves from those that do. For example, UKIP has rejected overtures to work with France's far-right, anti-EU, anti-immigration *Front National* because of its racist and anti-Semitic past, while *Front National* (which has been attempting to reinvent itself) has asserted that it would not work with parties that it considers to be neo-Nazi, such as Hungary's *Jobbik* and Greece's Golden Dawn.

The European Parliament 37

While some recent press reports claim that a new prospective hardline "European Alliance for Freedom" may have enough MEPs from enough EU member states to form a political group, most observers believe it is not yet a done deal. Analysts also point out that even if the hardline euroskeptics can forge a political group in the next EP and form voting alliances with the ECR, the EFD, and some nonattached members, they will still be a collective minority. The EPP and the S&D combined are expected to retain a clear majority of roughly 400 seats. Even a fully united euroskeptic front would have to gain the support of other political groups to block legislation, and most experts assert that it is unlikely that they could create wholesale gridlock.[11]

Others assert that regardless of whether the hardline euroskeptics are able to form a political group, their presence in the EP could have still some significant implications. With or without a group, hardliners could use the EP as a venue from which to espouse their anti-EU views— thereby threatening current EU efforts to restore public faith in the EU project in the wake of the Eurozone crisis—and as a platform from which to advance themselves in national politics in their home countries. In addition, some analysts suggest that the euroskeptic parties (on both the right and left) could shift certain EU economic and social policies if they prompt mainstream EP political groups and established EU leaders to embrace similar positions in order to protect their own national bases of support. Such political dynamics could produce a greater emphasis in the next EP and in the EU more generally on economic growth rather than austerity measures, tighter EU immigration policies, and slower progress toward further EU enlargement or integration.[12]

The EP President

Every two-and-a-half years (twice per parliamentary term), MEPs vote to elect a President of the European Parliament. The majority coalition in the EP (previously and currently an unofficial "Grand Coalition" between the EPP and the Socialists) has traditionally agreed to split the position of EP president over each five-year term. At the opening session of the current EP in mid-July 2009, Members elected Polish MEP Jerzy Buzek of the EPP as President for the first half of the 2009-2014 parliamentary term. Buzek, a former prime minister of Poland, was the first ever EP President from one of the Central and Eastern European countries that joined the EU in 2004. In January 2012, German MEP Martin Schulz of S&D took over as EP President for the second half of the EP's current term. Schulz has been an MEP since 1994 and was the leader of S&D until his election as EP President.

The President of the EP represents the Parliament externally and in relations with the other EU institutions. The President oversees the work of the Parliament and is responsible for ensuring that its rules of procedure are followed. The President is assisted in managing the Parliament's internal organization and affairs by a Conference of Presidents (composed of the EP President and the chairs of the political groups) and by a Bureau (composed of 14 Vice-Presidents and five Quaestors, responsible for administrative and financial matters). The signature of the EP President is the final step in approval of the EU budget, and the EP President cosigns, together with the appropriate representative of the Council of Minister's rotating presidency, legislation adopted under the co-decision procedure.

Committees

The EP has 20 standing committees, each addressing specific issues such as education, the environment, and economic and monetary affairs. The EP may also set up subcommittees and special committees, which investigate or oversee specific issues for a limited period of time. For example, in 2006, the EP established a special committee to examine the role of EU member states in hosting secret CIA detention facilities and aiding CIA flights related to the rendition of terrorism suspects. Only the EP's foreign affairs committee currently has subcommittees (one focuses on human rights, the other on security and defense issues).

EP committees vary in size, usually containing from 20 to 80 MEPs. Each committee has a chairman, four vice-chairmen, and a secretariat to guide its work. The political makeup of the committees reflects that of the EP as a whole, and committee posts are allocated proportionally to the respective size of the political groups; for example, the EPP currently chairs eight committees, the S&D six, and the ALDE two.

EP committees are key actors in the adoption of EU legislation. In terms of their importance and strength, EP committees rival those in the U.S. Congress and surpass the role of committees in most national European legislatures. EP committees consider legislative proposals put forward by the Commission and the Council of Ministers. The appropriate committee (e.g., the Committee on the Environment, Public Health, and Food Safety would deal with legislation on pollution) appoints a MEP as "rapporteur" to draft a

The European Parliament   39

report on the legislative proposal under consideration. The rapporteur submits a draft report to the committee for discussion, which the committee then votes on and possibly amends. The committee's report is then considered in a plenary session of the entire Parliament, amended if necessary, and put to a vote. The EP thus adopts its position on the proposed EU legislation. Committees may also draw up their "own initiative" reports, in which they recommend action in a particular area by the Commission or the member states.

Delegations

The European Parliament plays a role in the EU's international presence through a total of 41 delegations that range in size; most have between 20 and 50 MEPs. These delegations maintain parliament-to-parliament contacts and relations with representatives of many countries and regions around the world. For example, the EP has interparliamentary delegations for relations with the United States and the NATO Parliamentary Assembly, as well as with Russia, Iran, Israel, the Palestinian Legislative Council, China, India, and the Korean Peninsula.

Administration

A Secretariat of almost 5,000 nonpartisan civil servants provides administrative and technical support to the Parliament. In addition, MEPs and political groups have their own staffs.

Location and Schedule

Strasbourg, France (near the German border), is the official seat of the EP; plenary sessions are held there for one week a month. For two weeks a month, the EP's standing committees meet 300 miles to the northwest in Brussels, Belgium, where the European Commission and the Council of Ministers are located. There are also occasional "part plenary" sessions (two days) in Brussels.

One week each month is set aside for meetings of the political groups, which are usually held in Brussels. MEPs must have offices and lodgings in both cities. The EP's Secretariat is based in both Brussels and Luxembourg, which is about mid-way between Strasbourg and Brussels.

Languages

Simultaneous interpretation of all parliamentary and committee debates is provided in the EU's 24 official languages. All parliamentary documents are translated into 22 of these languages (Irish and Maltese are sometimes excepted), and some documents must be translated into all 24. Such extensive translation and publication services represent significant administrative costs. However, many EU and EP officials consider such costs to be a price worth paying, both on democratic grounds—to enable MEPs to scrutinize and vote on draft EU laws in the languages they understand best—and on grounds of cultural and linguistic diversity within the Union.

GROWING INFLUENCE AND ONGOING CHALLENGES

As noted previously, EP advocates assert that "co-decision" and its institutional supervisory roles have substantially enhanced the Parliament's influence. The Lisbon Treaty, in effect, gives the EP veto authority over the vast majority of EU legislation and a greater say over the EU's budget. In addition, the Lisbon Treaty gives the EP the right to approve or reject all international agreements by a simple majority and expands the EP's decision-making authority over trade-related issues. Analysts observe that the EP has not been shy about exerting its new powers under the Lisbon Treaty. Over the last two years, for example, the annual budget negotiations between the EP and the Council of Ministers have gone down to the wire and MEPs are increasingly (and successfully) demanding greater input during the drafting and negotiation stages of the EU legislative process.

Supporters also claim that the EP's influence has been growing even in consultative areas, such as the EU's common foreign policy, where the "co-decision procedure" does not apply and where decisions rest largely with the member states. They maintain that the EP has become a forum for debate on international issues, and uses its power of consent on cooperation accords with third parties and Parliamentary resolutions to promote its views and highlight issues such as human rights. For example, many observers credit the EP's opposition in 2005 to ending the EU's arms embargo on China (on both human rights and strategic grounds) as one factor that eventually dissuaded member states from lifting the embargo. More recently, some experts assert that the agreement reached between the EP and the other EU institutions on the establishment of the European External Action Service (EEAS)—the new EU diplomatic corps called for by the Lisbon Treaty—has the potential to greatly increase the EP's voice in the foreign policy realm. The EP fought for and largely won considerable oversight of the EEAS by demanding scrutiny over its political appointments, staffing, and budget.

At the same time, a number of analysts suggest that the enhanced powers granted to the EP by the Lisbon Treaty, and the EP's resulting newfound assertiveness, could lead to greater interinstitutional rivalry. This could make the EU's legislative and decision-making processes even more complex as the EP, the European Commission, and the Council of Ministers all vie to protect their own institutional turf. For example, some observers contend that wrangling between the EP and the other EU institutions regarding the EEAS delayed its establishment. Others counter that a main aim of the Lisbon Treaty was to improve democratic accountability within the EU, and that the EP is merely seeking to defend its parliamentary prerogatives and the interests of EU citizens. As such, they view the debate among the various EU institutions over the establishment of the EEAS as part of the democratic process.

Despite the EP's new powers and growing influence following the Lisbon Treaty, the EP still faces several challenges of public perception. A November 2011 opinion poll found that 45% of people across all EU member states had a "neutral" opinion of the EP, but that 26% had a "negative" view (up 9 percentage points compared to a similar 2008 poll).[13] Some skeptics contend that the EP, despite being a directly elected body, lacks the legitimacy of national parliaments. They argue that the EU's legislative process is overly complex and often focused on highly technical issues, leading to a lack of public understanding about the role of the EP. Limited public awareness of the EP's activities, they maintain, is reflected in the consistently declining turnout in European Parliament elections. And while studies on voting behavior in the EP show that ideology holds greater influence than nationality (with MEPs voting with their party groups the vast majority of the time), many MEPs campaign for the European Parliament on national rather than European issues. Many voters also tend to view EP elections as national mid-term elections—an indication of voter opinion on the performance of the national government—rather than as a vote on Europe-wide issues.[14]

Another major concern is costs, which the EP has long been under public pressure to reduce. The fact that MEPs and their staffs regularly shuttle between three cities leads to sizeable travel and hotel bills; current outside estimates suggest that such commuting costs total roughly $285 million a year.[15] Yet, the suggestion that the EP should consolidate its operations in one city continues to meet with strong opposition in the host countries of France, Belgium, and Luxembourg, which fear the loss of symbolism and prestige, in addition to jobs and other economic benefits. The French city of Strasbourg, which is close to the German border, was originally chosen as the seat of the EP to serve as a symbol of peace and reconciliation between the two countries, and both argue it should continue to do so. Construction of multi-million-dollar buildings in Brussels and Strasbourg in the late 1990s to accommodate the growth in MEPs following the addition of 10 new members in 2004 also stirred public controversy.

In addition, the EP continues to battle against a "gravy train" image and charges that it lacks transparency. Until 2009, for example, the EP had a flat-rate expense regime and MEPs did not have to submit for reimbursement for business and travel expenses. Recently, the EP has been beset by a "cash-for-amendments" scandal, in which several MEPs have been accused of accepting money in exchange for introducing amendments on legislation pending in the EP. In response, the EP approved a new code of conduct in December 2011 aimed at tightening rules on MEPs' financial declarations and on their contacts with lobbyists. Critics contend, however, that the new code of conduct contains a number of loopholes, with MEPs still able to engage in some paid outside activities and permitted to accept certain gifts of hospitality without having to disclose them.[16]

THE UNITED STATES AND THE EUROPEAN PARLIAMENT

Implications of the EP's Evolution for U.S. Interests

Policy makers and analysts on both sides of the Atlantic assert that the European Parliament's enhanced powers following the entrance into force of the Lisbon Treaty in December 2009 has made the EP an increasingly important actor in the conduct of U.S.-EU relations. As noted previously, the EP has been keen to exert its new powers under the Lisbon Treaty, and this has had implications for U.S. interests, especially with respect to the approval of several U.S.-EU or international agreements. In February 2010, for example, by a vote of 378 to 196 (with 31 abstentions), the EP rejected a U.S.-EU accord aimed at countering terrorism; the so-called SWIFT agreement, negotiated by the European Commission and approved by the Council of Ministers, would have continued allowing U.S. authorities access to European financial data in an effort to help prevent or investigate terrorist attacks. Prior to the Lisbon Treaty, the EP did not have the authority to veto such an accord.

Observers attribute the EP's rejection of the U.S.-EU SWIFT accord to several factors. Many MEPs had long claimed that the U.S.-EU SWIFT agreement did not contain sufficient protections to safeguard the personal data and privacy rights of EU citizens; thus, many saw the "no" vote as unsurprising on substantive grounds. In addition, however, some MEPs reportedly sought to send a message to the Commission and Council, conveying that the EP's position—in light of the changes brought about by the Lisbon Treaty—must now be taken into account during (and not after) the negotiation of international agreements or the drafting of new legislative proposals. Although the EP eventually approved a revised U.S.-EU SWIFT agreement in July 2010, it did so only after several EP demands related to strengthening data privacy protections were agreed to by the United States, the European Commission, and the Council of Ministers.

Some experts also worried that another U.S.-EU anti-terrorism measure related to sharing Passenger Name Record (PNR) flight data might be rejected by the EP. Since 2004, the United States and the EU had concluded several agreements permitting airlines operating flights between Europe and the United States to provide U.S. counterterrorism and law enforcement authorities with PNR data. These PNR accords were controversial in Europe, and especially in the EP, because of privacy and data protection concerns. Until the Lisbon Treaty, however, the EP did not have a role in approving these accords.

After the Lisbon Treaty, it became evident that a PNR agreement dating from 2007, which had been provisionally in force, required EP approval (by majority vote) in order for it to remain in force. In December 2010, the Obama Administration agreed to renegotiate some elements of the 2007 PNR accord, largely in recognition of the fact that the EP was unlikely to approve the existing 2007 agreement. U.S.-EU negotiations on a revised PNR accord were concluded in November 2011. After some contentious debates, the EP approved the revised U.S.-EU PNR agreement in April 2012 (by a vote of 409 to 226, with 33 abstentions). U.S. officials assert that while the new PNR agreement includes several innovations aimed at meeting EP concerns and better safeguarding passengers' personal information, it also preserves and in some cases improves the accord's operational effectiveness.

EP concerns about data privacy have been heightened further in the wake of the June 2013 disclosures of U.S. National Security Agency surveillance programs, press reports suggesting that U.S. intelligence agencies have monitored EU diplomatic offices, and subsequent allegations of other U.S. intelligence operations in Europe (including reported phone record collection efforts in France and Spain as well as the past monitoring of German Chancellor Angela Merkel's mobile phone). Consequently, many analysts worry that future U.S.-EU information-sharing agreements may not be able to secure the necessary EP approval. The U.S.-EU SWIFT accord will be up for renewal in 2015, and the PNR agreement in 2019. EP approval will also be required for any eventual U.S.-EU data privacy and protection agreement (DPPA), under negotiation since 2011; the DPPA is intended to bridge U.S.-EU differences in the application of privacy rights and make the negotiation of future data-sharing accords easier in the law enforcement context.[17]

In response to the NSA programs and other spying allegations, the EP established a special working group (within the EP's civil liberties committee) to conduct an in-depth investigation into U.S. surveillance activities (as well as similar, related intelligence collection efforts by EU member states). The EP's working group was chaired by Claude Moraes, a British MEP from the S&D political group. In March 2014, the full Parliament adopted the so-called "Moraes report" (with 544 votes in favor, 78 opposed, and 60 abstentions), concluding the EP's inquiry into the alleged surveillance activities.[18]

The "Moraes report" is deeply critical of the NSA's alleged mass surveillance programs, as well as those purportedly carried out by the UK's signals intelligence agency, and asserts that such mass surveillance activities could have potentially severe implications on fundamental freedoms and the privacy rights of EU citizens. The report also contains a long list of recommendations, some of which pertain to U.S.-EU political, security, and economic relations. In particular, the report urges the United States to revise its legislation to recognize the privacy rights of EU citizens and to provide judicial redress; reiterates previous EP calls for the immediate suspension of the U.S.-EU SWIFT agreement and notes concerns about the PNR accord; and calls on the European Commission to suspend the U.S.-EU Safe Harbor agreement (which dates from 2000 and enables U.S. companies to process European customer data). The resolution approving the "Moraes report" is not binding on the European Commission or the member states, which do not appear inclined at present to take action against SWIFT; similarly, the Commission has rejected suspending Safe Harbor because, in its view, doing so could adversely affect EU and U.S. business interests. Nevertheless, the

"Moraes report" does express the "sense" of the Parliament on these issues, and thus carries a degree of political weight.

The alleged U.S. surveillance activities have also prompted MEPs to demand that EU data protection reforms, which have been under discussion in the EP since January 2012, include even stronger safeguards than those initially proposed by the European Commission for personal data transferred outside of the EU. In March 2014, the Parliament approved several changes to the Commission's proposal on data protection reforms that would essentially require U.S.-based Internet and social media companies to obtain the approval of European officials before complying with any U.S. warrants for the personal data of EU citizens; significant monetary fines would be imposed should companies fail to comply. U.S. officials and industry representatives are concerned that such provisions could impede U.S.-European law enforcement cooperation, be overly burdensome for U.S. businesses, and put U.S. firms in a difficult situation, in which they would be forced to choose between complying with U.S. legal demands for data and EU rules that may prohibit its transfer. The EP's version of the proposed data protection reforms, however, must still be approved by the EU member states.[19]

Meanwhile, a key U.S.-EU-led effort to protect intellectual property rights (IPR), especially as they apply in the digital environment, has been complicated by the EP. In July 2012, the EP rejected the Anti-Counterfeiting Trade Agreement (ACTA), by a vote of 478 to 39, with 168 abstentions. ACTA was negotiated over the course of three years by the United States, the EU, and several other countries to strengthen IPR protection and enforcement measures worldwide. MEPs opposed to ACTA cited concerns that it was too vague and could jeopardize civil liberties, including Internet free speech. The EP's rejection of ACTA prevents the EU and its member states from joining the agreement in its current form, and the accord's future prospects are unclear.[20]

In addition, EP approval will ultimately be required to allow a future U.S.-EU accord on a Transatlantic Trade and Investment Partnership (TTIP) to enter into force. The EP has strongly supported the TTIP concept as a way to boost economic growth and stimulate job creation on both sides of the Atlantic. U.S.-EU negotiations on TTIP were launched in July 2013. However, following the disclosures of the NSA surveillance programs and the other allegations of U.S. intelligence collection activities in Europe, MEPs have cautioned European Commission officials to ensure that EU data protection standards are not undermined by any potential measures agreed to as part of TTIP, such as those governing transatlantic trade in services delivered over the

Internet. The "Moraes report" also warns that the consent of the EP to the final TTIP agreement could be endangered if the United States does not take steps to address EU concerns about U.S. safeguards for EU citizens' personal data, and that EU data protection legislation cannot be deemed as a trade discrimination measure during the course of the TTIP negotiations.[21]

Congress-Parliament Relations

Ties between the European Parliament and the U.S. Congress date back to 1972, when a U.S. congressional delegation first visited the EP in Brussels and Luxembourg. Since then, with a few exceptions, congressional-EP exchanges have taken place twice a year, and have provided the opportunity for sustained dialogue. The U.S. Congress-EP exchange is the oldest and widely considered the most prestigious of the EP's interparliamentary dialogues.

In 1999, the EP and the U.S. Congress launched the Transatlantic Legislators' Dialogue (TLD) as their official response to the U.S.-EU commitment in the 1995 New Transatlantic Agenda to enhance parliamentary ties between the EU and the United States. With the TLD, the two sides have committed to regular meetings twice a year to discuss a wide range of topical political and economic issues. In the EP, the TLD is led by a chairman and EP participants in the semi-annual TLD meetings are drawn from the EP's Delegation for Relations with the United States. In Congress, the TLD is headed by a chair and vice-chair and U.S. participants are from the House only. The most recent TLD meeting took place March 24-26, 2014, in Washington, DC (the venue for the TLD usually alternates between the United States and Europe). However, some U.S. analysts observe that the TLD remains relatively obscure in Congress, with ambiguity regarding which Members actually belong, and no role given to the U.S. Senate.

Many MEPs would like to enhance cooperation with the U.S. Congress further. In March 2009, the EP adopted a resolution, which among other measures, asserted that the U.S. Congress and the EP should promote closer ties between legislative committees and should create a reciprocal legislative "early-warning" system to identify potential legislative activities that could affect relations between the United States and the EU. In January 2010, the EP established a liaison office with the U.S. Congress in Washington, DC; EP staffers deployed as part of this office seek to keep the EP better informed of legislative activity in the U.S. House and Senate by attending hearings,

The European Parliament 47

following legislation, and establishing working relationships with Members of Congress, committees, and their staffs.[22]

Especially in light of the EP's new powers as a result of the Lisbon Treaty, some U.S. officials and analysts suggest that it is in U.S. interests for Congress to forge stronger ties with the EP. Those of this view note that in the past, there have been instances in which legislation passed by either Congress or the EU has contributed to U.S.-EU tensions. In 2002, for example, U.S.-EU frictions surfaced over the Sarbanes-Oxley Act to reform corporate accounting practices; EU officials claimed that the U.S. legislation did not take into account differences in European corporate governance and financing mechanisms. More recently, U.S. officials and many Members of Congress have strongly objected to the inclusion of aviation in the EU's Emissions Trading System (ETS) and oppose its application to U.S. air carriers. Some experts assert that tensions over such issues could have perhaps been avoided—or at least reduced—if both sides' legislative bodies had consulted more ahead of time.

On the other hand, skeptics doubt the need to establish a closer relationship between Congress and the EP. They assert that structural and procedural differences could make effective legislative coordination difficult, and that there are some issues in which the EP may have a legislative say, but Congress does not, and vice-versa. For example, the EP had to give its consent to the U.S.-EU agreements on SWIFT and PNR, but these accords were not subject to equivalent congressional approval because they were negotiated by the United States as executive agreements under existing U.S. law. Others maintain, however, that even in matters in which only one side has a direct legislative role, closer ties and personal relationships between Members of Congress and their counterparts in the EP could help sway the debate and perhaps produce more favorable outcomes. Some believe that the proposed Transatlantic Trade and Investment Partnership, as well as data privacy issues, may help to heighten Congress-EP engagement in the years ahead.[23]

End Notes

[1] The 28 member states of the EU are Austria, Belgium, Bulgaria, Croatia, Cyprus, the Czech Republic, Denmark, Estonia, Finland, France, Germany, Greece, Hungary, Ireland, Italy, Latvia, Lithuania, Luxembourg, Malta, the Netherlands, Poland, Portugal, Romania, Slovakia, Slovenia, Spain, Sweden, and the United Kingdom.

[2] Prior to the entry into force of the Lisbon Treaty, the "consent procedure" was known as the "assent procedure."

[3] Currently, EU member states have set an annual budget ceiling of 1.23% of the Union's gross national income. The EU budget comes from three main sources: external customs duties; a share of each member state's value added tax (VAT) revenue; and a further contribution from each member state based on the size of its individual GNI.

[4] The level of commitment appropriations is the maximum value of commitments to pay future bills, whereas the payment appropriations is the actual amounts to pay for previous commitments.

[5] See Fact Sheets on the European Union, "The Budgetary Procedure," available on the website of the European Parliament, http://www.europarl.europa.eu.

[6] The EU's current multiannual financial framework covers the period 2014-2020.

[7] Barroso, from Portugal, is a former prime minister from a conservative Portuguese political party. As such, he was backed in both 2004 and 2009 for Commission President by the EP's largest political group, which is center-right in political orientation. See also, Sebastian Kurpas, "The Treaty of Lisbon: How Much 'Constitution' Is Left?," *CEPS Policy Brief*, December 2007.

[8] Prior to direct elections, MEPs were appointed by their national parliaments.

[9] Joshua Chaffin, "Europe: United By Hostility," *Financial Times*, October 15, 2013; Naftali Bendavid and Gabriele Parussini, "Anti-EU Parties Gather Strength in Europe," *Wall Street Journal*, January 1, 2014; "Latest Poll Predicts Tie in EU Parliament Race," EurActiv.com, March 20, 2014.

[10] "Voters Steer Europe to the Right," BBC News, June 8, 2009; Stephen Castle, "Far Right Is Left Out at EU's Assembly," *International Herald Tribune*, July 15, 2009; Julia De Clerck-Sachsse, "The New European Parliament: All Change or Business as Usual?," *CEPS Special Report*, August 2009.

[11] Andrew Higgins, "Right Wing's Surge in Europe Has the Establishment Rattled," *New York Times*, November 8, 2013; "Turning Right," *The Economist*, January 4, 2014; Cas Mudde, "The Le Pen-Wilders Alliance and the European Parliament," *Washington Post*, February 11, 2014; Thomas Seymat, "How the European Elections Could Redesign the Eurosceptic Landscape," Euronews.com, April 10, 2014.

[12] Naftali Bendavid and Gabriele Parussini, "Anti-EU Parties Gather Strength in Europe," *Wall Street Journal*, January 1, 2014; "Turning Right," *The Economist*, January 4, 2014; "Latest Poll Predicts Tie in EU Parliament Race," EurActiv.com, March 20, 2014.

[13] Eurobarometer, *Parlemeter 2011*; http://www.europarl.europa.eu/pdf/eurobarometre/2012/76-3/report_EN.pdf.

[14] Simon Hix and Abdul Noury, "After Enlargement: Voting Patterns in the Sixth European Parliament," *Legislative Studies Quarterly*, May 2009; Julia De Clerck-Sachsse and Piotr Maciej Kaczynski, "The European Parliament: More Powerful, Less Legitimate," *CEPS Working Document*, May 2009.

[15] As quoted in Suzanne Daley and Stephen Castle, "A Parliament on the Move Grows Costly," *New York Times*, June 28, 2011.

[16] "MEPs Approve New Code of Conduct," EurActiv.com, December 2, 2011; James Kanter, "Europeans Losing Faith in Their Parliament," *New York Times*, November 5, 2012.

[17] For more information on the SWIFT and PNR accords, and on the DPPA negotiations, see CRS Report RS22030, *U.S.-EU Cooperation Against Terrorism*, by Kristin Archick.

[18] European Parliament resolution P7_TA(2014)0230, adopted March 12, 2014, available at http://www.europarl.europa.eu. The full text of the "Moraes report" is contained in this resolution.

The European Parliament 49

[19] James Fontanella-Khan, "MEPs Call for Clause to Limit American Internet Snooping," *Financial Times*, June 19, 2013; Michael Birnbaum, "EU Fury on Allegations of U.S. Spying," *Washington Post*, June 30, 2013; European Parliament Press Release, "MEPs Tighten Up Rules To Protect Personal Data in the Digital Era," March 12, 2014.

[20] For more information, see CRS Report R41107, *The Proposed Anti-Counterfeiting Trade Agreement: Background and Key Issues*, by Shayerah Ilias Akhtar.

[21] For more information on TTIP, see CRS Report R43387, *Transatlantic Trade and Investment Partnership (TTIP) Negotiations*, by Shayerah Ilias Akhtar and Vivian C. Jones.

[22] European Parliament resolution A6-0114/2009, adopted March 26, 2009.

[23] For more information, see CRS Report R41552, *The U.S. Congress and the European Parliament: Evolving Transatlantic Legislative Cooperation*, by Kristin Archick and Vincent L. Morelli.

In: Democratic Credentials of the European Union ISBN: 978-1-63321-628-0
Editor: Evonne Graham   © 2014 Nova Science Publishers, Inc.

Chapter 3

THE EUROPEAN UNION: A DEMOCRATIC INSTITUTION?[*]

Vaughne Miller and Jon Lunn, with contributions by Steven Ayres

This paper asks questions about the democratic credentials of the European Union. The paper begins by looking at definitions of democracy and the historical development of democratic political systems. It then looks at the European Union's decision-making institutions and at a range of views from academics and politicians on the extent to which they conform to generally accepted norms of democratic government.

The paper acknowledges the EU's 'democratic deficit' and considers the causes of this. In the context of future EU Treaty reform, it considers possible remedies for the democratic deficit, including those proposed by the UK Government.

SUMMARY

In order to assess the European Union's democratic credentials, it is necessary first to define democracy. Of course, this is much easier said than

---

[*] This is an edited, reformatted and augmented version of Research Paper 14/25, published by the House of Commons Library (United Kingdom), April 29, 2014. It contains Parliamentary information licensed under the Open Parliament Licence v1.0.

done. Democracy is a complex and contested concept. Debate about its content and character may have originated in ancient Greece but it rages no less passionately today. There are arguably two primary types of democracy: direct democracy, in which all citizens directly participate in decision-making; and representative democracy, in which the power of the people is delegated to periodically elected representatives.

> "While the real, philosophical, ideal or essential meaning of democracy remains the same, the actual practice of democracy may be said to be in the eye of the beholder".
>
> Democracy and its practice: a general theory of democratic relativity, Daniel Tetteh Osabu- Kle, Carleton University, 2002

Today, liberal democracy, with its strong affinity with the principle of representation and link to markets in the economic sphere, has become the dominant conception of democracy. But it has often been subject to criticism for not doing enough to address inequalities of wealth and power in society. Debates about democracy today can be said to have crystallised around two main questions: Is representative democracy broken at the national level? Can democracy reinvigorate itself at the international level? On that second question, there have long been major political disagreements about how much power can or should reside at the international level and what the basis of its legitimacy should be. Which brings us back to the subject of this paper – the EU as a democratic institution.

The democratic legitimacy of the EU has long been questioned - more so as successive EU Treaty amendments have limited the legislative powers of Member State governments by removing the national veto in decision-making, increasing the use of qualified majority voting and expanding the policy areas in which the EU has a role. Treaty amendments have on the other hand also enhanced the powers of the European Parliament and national parliaments, and provided for citizen consultations on major policy initiatives.

In spite of the European Parliament's gains in legislative and oversight powers over the years, its relative weakness compared with the other decision-making bodies, the Council and Commission, as well as the low turnout for EP elections, tend to support the argument that, although it is directly elected, the EP also lacks democratic legitimacy.

The European Commission has long been criticised for being appointed rather than directly elected, and the Council for being secretive. Council

The European Union: A Democratic Institution? 53

transparency has been the subject of a number of reforms in the last two decades, which have resulted among other things in greater access to Council documents and Council sessions being opened to the public. A lso, the next appointment of the Commission President will be linked to the May 2014 EP elections in accordance with the 2009 *Treaty of Lisbon*.

New roles and powers for national parliaments in the EU decision-making process have not convinced national politicians that they have any real power to influence EU decisions. National parliaments are responsible for scrutinising their governments and EU business, but there are questions about the efficiency and quality of their scrutiny.

There are now more opportunities for citizens to influence the EU through petitions and the new 'citizens' initiative', but opinion polls indicate that these have not brought the EU much 'closer' to its citizens.

The UK Government believes national parliaments should have greater influence in EU decision-making, with a power of veto over EU legislative proposals. The Prime Minister intends to seek EU reforms that will put national parliaments in a stronger position in Europe.

1. DEFINING DEMOCRACY

1.1. Introduction

The meaning of 'democracy' is highly complex and, to this day, much contested.

Bullock and Stallybrass usefully define it as "the rule of the *demos*, the citizen body: the right of all to decide what are matters of general concern."[1]

Useful as this definition is, it leaves many questions unanswered. Who is included within the *demos*? How are decisions best made? What should be deemed matters of general concern? Is democracy fundamentally rooted in the state?

The same uncertainties arise whichever definition you propose – even that great democratic clarion call with the greatest popular reach: 'rule of the people, by the people, for the people'. In what follows, we do our best to explore these uncertainties and, by so doing, lay some foundations for our subsequent discussion of the European Union (EU) as a democratic institution.

1.2. Typology of Democracy

There are arguably two primary types of democracy in the world today – although some make a case for including a third.

The first primary type is ***direct democracy*** – in which all citizens directly participate in decision-making. It is the oldest type, originating in Ancient Greece. The scope of Athenian citizenry did not extend to women, slaves and foreigners, but much more inclusive versions of the idea have been attempted in the modern era.[2] Referendums are an example of direct democracy today.

The other primary type is ***representative democracy***, in which the power of the people is delegated to representatives periodically elected by them, who then assemble to make decisions on their behalf, usually through majority voting.[3] Representative democracy is viewed as being part-and-parcel of a political order involving checks and balances, in which other key institutions such as the judiciary and the media also limit the power of government, where necessary challenging its decisions and actions. This is undoubtedly the dominant conception of democracy today.

A possible third primary type – perhaps the least familiar to people – is ***associational democracy***, in which collective non-state bodies become involved in political decision- making. Examples of such organisations today are trades unions, human rights groups and business associations. Aware that some critics view democracies as vulnerable to lobbying --or worse still, 'capture' – by powerful interests, advocates of associational democracy are keen to stress that, under the right conditions, it can be a powerful force for good as well as for ill.[4]

It is important to note that each of these types of democracy can be expressed across a wide spectrum, running from 'minimalist' at one end to 'maximalist' at the other – for example, direct democracy can involve an occasional referendum on the one hand, or a model based on almost perpetual participation on the other; representative democracy can sometimes extend to little more than periodic voting in a context where checks and balances barely exist in practice. Depending on where a person places themselves on this spectrum, views on whether a democracy is suffering from a 'deficit' – or, indeed, has even ceased to be democratic – will vary widely. Such considerations are also relevant today in debates about 'democratisation' – where countries undertake a transition from authoritarianism to democracy.[5]

1.3. Genealogy of Democracy

Like all the central ideas shaping political society today, democracy has plenty of histori cal baggage. Democracy as an idea and practice had its origins in ancient Greece. However, even at its birth there were different and ambiguous definitions in play, ranging from a definition familiar to us today, 'rule of the people, by the people, for the people' (often ascribed to Cleon), to 'all that is opposed to despotic power' (Thucydides), to 'a state where the freemen and the poor, being in the majority are invested with the power of the state' (Aristotle).[6]

During the medieval period and subsequently in Europe, the predominant meaning of democracy was, according to Raymond Williams, drawn from Thomas Aquinas, "who defined democracy as popular power, where the ordinary people, by force of numbers, governed – oppressed – the rich, the whole people acting like a tyrant." He argues that this meaning remained powerful until well into the 19th century and was used in the main as an argument *against* democracy because of the threat popular power might pose to property and security.[7]

Some academics have argued that the emergence from the mid-19th century onwards of representative democracy in which the representatives were entitled to be part of an assembly by virtue of having been elected by increasingly large sections of the population, was in part a defensive response by ruling elites to the growing threat from forms of popular power.[8] Often under pressure from mass protests, representative democracies gradually extended the vote to larger groups of people: adult middle class men were first to gain the vote, followed eventually by working class men – and then ultimately, women.

But the supporters of representative democracy also had positive arguments they could make. Direct democracy, they argued, could not work in more complex, large-scale societies. For them, what the enemies of property and security failed to take into account was the fact that all men (and in due course, women and children too) have natural rights, over which untrammelled popular power, all too often manipulated by demagogues, can simply ride roughshod, with potentially disastrous consequences for a society.[9]

A philosophy and practice of *liberal democracy,* with a strong affinity with the principle of representation, gradually emerged from the 18th century onwards in opposition to this vision. This emergent philosophy placed political democracy within a set of restraining checks and balances in which the principle of periodic free election of representatives to a rule -based assembly was paramount. In the economic realm, markets were to be the capillaries of a free society.[10]

Nonetheless, some 19th century critics of liberal democracy rejected it on the grounds that the commitment to political equality did not extend sufficiently into the economic realm, stopping at equality of opportunity – well short of equality of outcome. Seeking to reconnect democracy with more radical conceptions of the term, many such critics were behind the rise of alternative political ideologies, including social democracy, out of which ultimately sprang a host of 'reformist' and revolutionary parties of the Left. However, during the 20th century, once in power, revolutionary parties of the Left abandoned political democracy, substituting themselves for 'the people', ostensibly in pursuit of maximum economic equality. Techniques of both direct democracy and representative democracy were deployed and abused to sustain those parties in power indefinitely in these 'people's democracies'.[11]

20th century supporters of liberal democracy countered that it was perfectly possible under its aegis to address issues of wealth and power in society through a combination of markets and political action. More broadly, they insisted that it was a superior means of resolving the inevitable conflicts that arise between different groups in society in ways that all those groups would accept as legitimate – or, in the case of those who might have lost out, at least tolerate – on the grounds that their representatives might one day be in the majority in parliament and government and be able to shape decision-making in their favour.[12]

For at least 30 years after the end of the Second World War in 1945, most mainstream European parties across the political spectrum effectively endorsed a marriage of liberal and reformist social democracy in which associational variants (sometimes characterised as 'corporatism') gained significant ground. Of course, revolutionaries of the Left always viewed the positive case for liberal democracy as naive at best or self -serving at worst. But the fall of the Berlin Wall in 1989 heralded the collapse of most of the self-proclaimed people's democracies and the marginalisation for a prolonged period of radical socialist politics. However, those who continue to adhere to this form of politics have argued that, since it was deprived of its historic enemy, the marriage of liberal democracy and reformist social democracy has come under strain; for them, the market has increasingly come to govern the state, generating a political economy of 'neo-liberalism' that is destructive of democracy.[13] Since the 2007/08 global financial crisis, elements of this argument have got a hearing within more mainstream circles.[14]

The European Union: A Democratic Institution? 57

To sum up, over the centuries there has been a distinct reversal of fortune between the two main types of democracy identified earlier in our typology. Whereas until the 19th century, direct democracy was the predominant (but often negatively viewed) understanding of democracy, today it has been rendered relatively marginal by representative democracy, whose liberal variant is apparently now in the ascendant. The purchase on the human imagination of direct democracy has never been entirely extinguished. It has survived co - option by totalitarian governments over the past century and, indeed, has continued to operate in some form or other within many representative democracies. But it still carrie s a whiff of danger about it.

1.4. Power, Accountability, Legitimacy and Sovereignty

By now it should be clear that there are a number of closely related political concepts which must also be addressed in order to enhance our understanding of the meaning(s) of democracy. Arguably amongst the most important of these concepts are *power* (some might prefer to use its synonym, authority), *accountability*, *legitimacy* and *sovereignty*.

Power
All forms of government involve the exercise of power by some people over others. As a concept and in practice, power has no intrinsic relationship to democracy. Power can be, and has often been, exercised absolutely and without limit, whether under absolute monarchies in the past or totalitarian states more recently. However, supporters of all types of democracy assert that one of its great virtues is precisely that it places limits upon the exercise of power through systems of checks and balances between different branches of government that have independence from each other.[15] Supporters of democracy also claim that these systems of checks and balances increase the effectiveness of power whenever it is exercised.[16]

Accountability
Although forms of accountability can be found in political systems that may not qualify as democratic, supporters of democracy promote it as both the most desirable and effective means of ensuring accountability between citizens and those who hold power. It does so in essence by providing citizens with means (voting in elections) of removing those who hold power at their behest.[17] By extension, this generates an incentive for power-holders to create,

or at the very least acquiesce in, structures and processes of scrutiny and oversight (for example, parliaments and the media) through which their performance may be evaluated during periods when their electoral fate is not on the line. It follows from this argument that crucial preconditions for democratic accountability are official openness and transparency.[18]

Legitimacy

The legitimacy of a political and social system arises from the willingness of people to obey those who hold power because they have sufficient faith or trust in them. As with the concept of accountability, legitimacy can exist in non-democratic contexts, but advocates of democracy claim that freely and fairly electing those who hold power it is the most desirable and effective means of creating and sustaining legitimacy. Indeed, some of them go on to argue how well a democracy functions in practice can become an important test of the legitimacy of those in power. Nonetheless, even in well-established democracies, other bases for legitimacy, such as 'tradition' or the charisma of particular leaders, can remain influential.[19] But it is not just political freedoms that bestow legitimacy. The vast majority of believers in the virtues of democracy also accept that, unless it also delivers a sufficient level of socio-economic benefit over time to sections of the population, its ability to create and sustain legitimacy will be damaged.

Sovereignty

Debate about the meaning of sovereignty has been no less fierce than debate about democracy itself. Sovereignty is about where and with whom power fundamentally resides. Its origins lie in kingship, or the rule of the sovereign. However, over the centuries it has become largely depersonalised. Today, sovereignty is often viewed as residing in three main – sometimes overlapping, sometimes conflicting – locations: in the people, in the state and/or in the nation.

Popular Sovereignty

Unlike in the past, popular sovereignty is today largely used interchangeably with the concept of democracy, embodied by the mantra: 'of the people, for the people, by the people'. But as we have already seen, agreeing what constitutes popular sovereignty is an altogether less straightforward matter.[20]

State Sovereignty[21]

State sovereignty has a complex and ambiguous relationship to democracy which has changed a lot over time. State sovereignty operates in two contexts: within a state and in relation to the rest of the world.

Within a state, where it is primarily expressed through popular (including parliamentary) sovereignty, its orientation is clearly democratic. But this has only become common over the last century. Prior to that, state sovereignty had little relationship to democracy.

When it comes to relations between states, state sovereignty is at first sight even less closely linked to democracy. Firstly, the *demos* may be hard to find (or create). Secondly, it is much more often the executive rather than the legislature (or some other form of popular power) that "acts as a sovereign" in the wider world.[22]

Nonetheless, many believe today that there is an increasingly strong relationship between the two as a result of the evolution of international law.[23] The Westphalian state system that emerged during the 16th and 17th centuries established the principle of equality between sovereigns. It can be argued that, in doing so, it planted the seeds for the later emergence of 'democratic elements' within that system, which can be summed up by the phrase 'international cooperation'.

Today, internationally recognised states have legal equality within the global order. This sometimes extends to equal voting rights in multilateral bodies – for example, at the United Nations General Assembly. In practice, some states have much greater weight in world affairs than others and this is sometimes reflected by unequal voting powers in such bodies – for example, the World Bank.

There has long been debate about the extent to which international cooperation between sovereign states violates the concept of popular sovereignty. There does not appear to be an inherent incompatibility. However, matters inevitably become less clear-cut if and when international cooperation between sovereign states begins to produce international institutions which aspire to a direct popular mandate of their own. The relationship of democratic states to such international institutions is unlikely to be simple or straightforward, given the dual loyalties this creates. It raises questions of whether – and if so, how far – sovereignty can be limited or divided. The EU is a pioneer in this regard.

Since the end of World War II, there have been important, if sometimes controversial, developments in international law that have made it increasingly difficult for sovereign states simply to ignore democratic principles. According to Besson, these originated in the desire of Western democracies to strengthen their own domestic legitimacy:

> Post-1945, international law was seen by modern democracies as a new way to secure their democratic development. Given the lack of consensus on minimal democratic requirements and in view of the intricate relationship between human rights and democracy, entrenching human rights protection from the outside through minimal international standards became the way to guarantee their new democratic regimes. International sovereignty objectively limited in this way became, in other words, a direct way to secure domestic sovereignty in a legitimate fashion. As a result, modern democratic sovereignty now finds its source both in constitutional and international law. Seen differently, the sovereigns behind international law are peoples within States, and no longer States only. And these peoples organize and constrain their sovereignty through both the international and domestic legal orders.[24]

Following the end of the Cold War in 1989, there has been a growing impulse within significant parts of the international community to consider that serious humanitarian abuses trump state sovereignty and legitimise external interference in a country's internal affairs. In this context, democratic inadequacies tend to be translated into the language of democracy's close cousin, human rights.[25]

Finally, there have also been occasional attempts in recent decades to create 'communities of democratic states' that will act in concert to promote their values amongst non - democracies or countries in transition to democracy. Predictably, non-democracies have resisted such initiatives - but some non-Western democracies (for example, India) that continue to place a high premium on state sovereignty have also been reluctant to become involved.[26]

National Sovereignty

This term is often used today virtually interchangeably with state sovereignty, although historically not all self-declared nations have necessarily had their 'own' internationally recognised state, or accepted the legitimacy of the one that contained them. Nevertheless, much of the discussion above about state sovereignty can also be taken to app ly to national sovereignty.

1.5. Contemporary Debates About Democracy

Before launching into the main body of this paper, we first briefly explore two of the most important wider debates about democracy taking place today. Both of them have significant ramifications for an assessment of the EU's democratic credentials.

Is Representative Democracy Broken at the National Level?
Despite the fact that it remains the dominant type of democracy today, critics of representative democracy at the national level have been on the increase in recent times.

Critiques of national-level representative democracy today include:

- A professional 'political class' has emerged, often having little in common with those they represent;[27]
- As power has shifted elsewhere, including to supranational bodies, national representatives have become increasingly ineffective in holding governments to account;[28]
- Powerful lobbies in society have established undue influence over national representatives – to the point where some have been captured by those interests. Trades unions and large corporations have been cited as cases in point;[29]
- There has been a collapse of party loyalties amongst voters and the dominant response to national politicians has become 'a plague on all their houses'; as a result voter turn-out in elections is often in decline.[30]

This is not the place to assess the validity of such critiques, which are often interlinked. However, their growing currency has encouraged supporters of greater direct democracy – who can be found across the political divide – to hope that it might experience a revival.

The defenders of representative democracy counter that deficiencies can be overcome through appropriate reforms – for example, by opening up opportunities to people from a wider range of backgrounds to become an MP, returning powers to parliament and improving scrutiny, more regular resort to referendums; better use of social media; and by giving constituents the power to recall parliamentarians.[31]

However, a radical minority – sometimes with links to the anti-capitalist Left – is sceptical about whether reform of this kind will be enough and is open to dramatically different ways of organising political and economic life, including by experimenting with highly participatory techniques of direct democracy. However, tensions have arisen over how to sustain such initiatives. Given its apparently strong propensity to produce hierarchies, a high degree of institutionalisation is viewed with considerable ambivalence by radical activists and thinkers.[32]

Can Democracy Reinvigorate Itself at the International Level?

Contemporary debates about representative democracy at the national level also have international implications.

Over the last 30 years or so, many democrats have come to the view that po liticians are increasingly unable to exercise power effectively within and through states. Those who take this view contend that economic globalisation, which has been accompanied by the rise of influential non-state actors such as multinational companies and international NGOs, means that politics must operate beyond the national level. In their view, many policy challenges today require growing international cooperation. They accept that this co-operation inevitably involves some transfer (or loan) of state sovereignty but believe that this is more than compensated for by the power that flows back from being part of a group of countries that operates in concert. This means that sovereignty need not necessarily be considered 'lost'.[33]

There is widespread acceptance today that international cooperation may in some circumstances take permanent institutional form and be imbued with certain degrees of power, but there remain major disagreements about how much power can or should reside at the international level and what the basis of its legitimacy should be.

For some, international institutions receive their mandate mainly from governments that are elected by the people at the level of the state. As such, democracy remains fundamentally rooted in the state and international cooperation should therefore be primarily intergovernmental in nature.[34]

But others argue that some international institutions may embody a more ambitious vision and require deeper political transformations. In these circumstances, while it is accepted that long-standing interests and identities remain important, new ones are created by these institutions which in due course justify higher levels of integration. Where this is so, such integration means that the issue of democratic representation must be addressed. State-level representatives will be unable effectively to hold such institutions to account. The solution, then, could be the establishment of international assemblies of representatives specifically elected for this purpose and other forms of direct accountability to citizens. [35] Those who make arguments for this kind of 'international liberal democracy' often describe themselves as "cosmopolitans". [36]

Such debates are highly germane in the case of the European Parliament, which shifted in 1979 from being an assembly of national parliamentarians to one in which representatives were directly elected in elections held in each member-state. At the same time, it is important to bear in mind that the EU is a unique case; to our knowledge, no other existing international institution has yet introduced direct elections to its own assembly. Those who believe democracy remains fundamentally rooted in the state are highly sceptical about the arguments made for direct elections to the European Parliament at the international level. This particular debate is dealt with in much more depth in the main body of this paper, so we will not expand on it here.

As we have seen, liberal cosmopolitans naturally favour international cooperation, including degrees of democratic integration where possible and appropriate. This can include elements of direct democracy. However, there are more radical currents of cosmopolitanism that go further, seeing a deeper, more fully democratised international cooperation as ess ential to changing unfair power relations within the global order. [37]

Those who take this view complain that international cooperation has hitherto often been characterised by elite control and manipulation, with ordinary people at best largely passive beneficiaries. Views of this kind are, of course, also sometimes held by defenders of state sovereignty on the right of the political spectrum. But more radical cosmopolitans often go further, claiming that there is a 'elite project' specifically driven by corp orations and the financial markets, and that many international institutions, as currently configured, have become the vehicles through which harsh measures are enforced that disproportionately affect the poor and vulnerable in society. Their solution is not to return to the state as the primary location of democracy but to strengthen international cooperation on a democratic basis through the deeper empowerment and participation of ordinary people. [38] While not dismissive of representative democracy, more radical cosmopolitans today tend to be attracted to direct democracy.

This viewpoint is in some ways a reiteration at the international level of the critiques by the anti-capitalist Left of representative democracy at the national level described above, although some reformist social democrats might also support aspects of this critique. The critique is nearly always internationalist in nature because its supporters strongly believe that no single country can succeed in promoting popular empowerment and participation on its own. Although its resonance increased following the 2007/08 global financial crisis, it remains a very much a minority perspective for now.

2. WHAT KIND OF UNION IS THE EUROPEAN UNION?

One of the problems in evaluating the democratic legitimacy of the EU is doing so against a valid benchmark when there is not one single template for what a democracy is (see section 1 above) and because "the meaning of democracy has also changed and evolved over time".[39] Another is that the EU is not a state, although it has many of the features of a state, and its members are not sub-state regions but sovereign states themselves. It is a supranational union of sovereign states. The 2009 German Federal Constitutional Court ruling on the compatibility of the *Treaty of Lisbon* with the German Constitution confirmed this status, providing a useful context for the discussion of the EU's democratic credentials:

> With the present status of integration, the European Union does, even upon the entry into force of the Treaty of Lisbon, not yet attain a shape that corresponds to the level of legitimisation of a democracy constituted as a state. It is not a federal state but remains an association of sovereign states to which the principle of conferral applies. [40]

"A system may benefit from a reasonably high level of legitimacy while not conforming to key features of democracy and vice versa. However, in the western tradition of liberal democracy, legitimacy and democracy are closely related".

Brigid Laffan , "Democracy and the European Union",1999

According to the literature, the EU falls short of being democratically legitimate in many areas, but, as Sonia Piedrafita (Centre for European Policy Studies) points out, "Political legitimacy is a very contentious concept when referring to non-state entities such as the EU".[41] Micossi notes that, as the EU is not a state, "comparisons with state-type models of democratic legitimisation may well prove misleading". Brigid Laffan has written that "political theorists have tended to focus on democracy and legitimacy in the traditional nation-state, rather than non-state forms of political order" and "The

EU is a challenge to how we conceptualize democracy, authority and legitimacy in contemporary politics".[42]

In terms of its structure and operation, the EU is not a straightforward inter-governmental organisation like the UN and it is not a federal entity like the United States. Sergio Fabrini[43] does not think either the intergovernmental or the fully federal model would work for the EU and that an EU integration strategy should focus on "amore satisfactory balance between the interests of states and those of citizens". To achieve this, Fabrini thinks:

> Europe needs political leaders who are able to look beyond these two strategies, who are aware that an intergovernmental union can never be a political union, and, at the same time, have also grasped that a federal union is not a federal state.[44]

The EU has dimensions of both a confederation and a federation. According to Michael Burgess's[45] analysis, the EU is "neither a federation nor a confederation in the classical sense", but "the European political and economic elites have shaped and moulded the EC/EU into a new form of international organization, namely, a species of 'new' confederation".[46] Joseph Weiler[47] thinks the EU has "charted its own brand of constitutional federalism".[48] Helen Wallace describes the EU system as a "contest ... between a loosely intergovernmental system, enabling member states to cooperate as a consortium, and tight supranationalism, based on autonomous European institutions" where "different institutional arrangements operate for different policy domains at different points across this spectrum".[49] In other words it is a kind of compromise of competing and complementary systems and arrangements. As the EU has expanded from six to 28 Members, the institutional structure has evolved but has remained constrained by opposing forces that have resulted in compromises and a degree of stability. Laurent Pech comments:

> ... institutional change in the EU continues to be largely shaped by antagonistic interests and philosophies (e.g., supranationalism v. intergovernmentalism, enhanced democratisation v. preservation of national sovereignty, interests of small countries v. those of large countries), and compromises must be constantly sought to guarantee the unanimous ratification of any new treaty by the Member States. The co-existence of these contrasting interests and philosophies largely explains why the Union's institutional framework has shown a high degree of stability over the years.[50]

Some governments, headed by the current UK one, would like an altogether different kind of EU and a different relationship between the EU and its Member State governments and parliaments. The following sections look at the democratic dimensions of the EU system, the so-called 'democratic deficit' and suggestions as to how this could be remedied. UK views are discussed in Section 6 of this paper.

2.1. The EU Aspires to be Democratic

The EU does not conform fully to any of the definitions of democracy in Section 1 of this paper, although it has elements of representative, direct and associational democracy. Just as there are a number of competing models of democracy, so there are within the EU system a number of competing models, systems, roles and principles. The EU has evolved as a hybrid system straddling the national and the transnational.[51] It is unique - sui generis - not homogeneous socially or culturally; politically only in so far as all Member States are deemed to be themselves democratic.

THE LAEKEN DECLARATION

"The European Union derives its legitimacy from the democratic values it projects, the aims it pursues and the powers and instruments it possesses.

However, the European project also derives its legitimacy from democratic, transparent and efficient institutions. The national parliaments also contribute towards the legitimacy of the European project (emphasis added). The declaration on the future of the Union, annexed to the Treaty of Nice, stressed the need to examine their role in European integration."

After the negative Danish referendum on the Maastricht Treaty in 1992, the subsequent Treaty amendment negotiations leading to the Amsterdam Treaty (1997) focused on institutional reforms and citizenship rights, in an attempt to make the EU more relevant and accessible to its citizens. The Commission's White Paper on Governance[52] in July 2001 referred to the EU's "double democratic mandate through a Parliament representing EU citizens and a Council representing the elected governments of the Member States". The EU, it stated, had achieved "by democratic means" fifty years of stability, peace and economic prosperity, high standards of living, an internal market and a strengthened Union voice in the world.[53] However, the White Paper and the Laeken Declaration on the Future of the European Union of the same year emphasised the democratic challenge facing the EU. At Laeken in December 2001 Member State governments concluded that there was an urgent need to increase the democratic legitimacy and transparency of the EU's institutions, to improve their efficiency in an enlarged Union, and to better associate the national parliaments with the EU's decision-making process.

> The first question is thus how we can increase the democratic legitimacy and transparency of the present institutions, a question which is valid for the three institutions.
>
> How can the authority and efficiency of the European Commission be enhanced? How should the President of the Commission be appointed: by the European Council, by the European Parliament or should he be directly elected by the citizens? Should the role of the European Parliament be strengthened? Should we extend the right of co-decision or not? Should the way in which we elect the members of the European Parliament be reviewed? Should a European electoral constituency be created, or should constituencies continue to be determined nationally? Can the two systems be combined? Should the role of the Council be strengthened? Should the Council act in the same manner in its legislative and its executive capacities? With a view to greater transparency, should the meetings of the Council, at least in its legislative capacity, be public? Should citizens have more access to Council documents? How, finally, should the balance and reciprocal control between the institutions be ensured?
>
> A second question, which also relates to democratic legitimacy, involv es the role of national parliaments. Should they be represented in a new institution, alongside the Council and the European Parliament? Should they have a role in areas of European action in which the European Parliament has no competence? Should they focus on the division of competence between Union and Member States, for example through preliminary checking of compliance with the principle of subsidiarity?

The third question was about how the EU could "improve the efficiency of decision -making and the workings of the institutions in a Union of some thirty Member States". What Laeken did not identify as a problem, let alone seek to tackle, was how the answers to the first two questions could be reconciled with the answer to the third.

The Lisbon Treaty which came into force in December 2009 (and before Lisbon the failed EU Constitutional Treaty) sought amongst other things to improve both the efficiency and the democratic legitimacy of the EU. While many argue that Lisbon has significantly strengthened democracy and legitimacy in the EU, others think Lisbon increased efficiency at the expense of democracy.[54]

2.2. EU Treaty Guarantees

The European Union Treaties as amended by Lisbon comprise the *Treaty on European Union* (TEU) and the *Treaty on the Functioning of the European Union* (TFEU), which together form the constitutional basis of the EU. Like many state constitutions they set out *inter alia* an institutional framework for the way the EU operates, a set of principles by which it will act, provisions on where powers and competences lie, and rules on how these things can be changed.

Article 4(1)TEU states that "competences not conferred upon the Union in the Treaties remain with the Member States", confirming the presumption in the 'subsidiarity principle' set out in Article 5(2)TEU that:

> ... the Union shall act only within the limits of the competences conferred upon it by the Member States in the Treaties to obtain the objectives set out therein. Competences not conferred upon the Union in the Treaties shall remain with the Member States.

The EU has no competences by right and no "competence-competence" (i.e. it cannot decide its own competences). The Court of Justice of the EU (CJEU) supervises this principle and acts on alleged breaches of it.55 But the Court has been accused of judicial activism in its willingness to promote the interests of the EU and EU integration, sometimes to the detriment of the interests of the Member States, and in the 1960s and 1970s established doctrines such as 'direct effect' and the primacy of EU law (see below) that are now the basis for the legal relationship between the EU and the Member States.

The EU Treaties aspire to create a democratic foundation for the Union. Article 10 TEU requires that EU action is founded on "representative democracy" (for definition see section 1 above).

> 1. The functioning of the Union shall be founded on representative democracy.

The European Union: A Democratic Institution? 69

2. Citizens are directly represented at Union level in the European Parliament.
    Member States are represented in the European Council by their Heads of State or Government and in the Council by their governments, themselves democratically accountable either to their national Parliaments, or to their citizens.
3. Every citizen shall have the right to participate in the democratic life of the Union. Decisions shall be taken as openly and as closely as possible to the citizen.
4. Political parties at European level contribute to forming European political awareness and to expressing the will of citizens of the Union.

This Article formalises the concept that the heads of state and government in the European Council and government ministers in the Council are themselves democratically accountable to their national parliaments or to their citizens. The Treaties thereby link democratic legitimacy at EU level to accountability and legitimacy at national level: democratic legitimacy is not just a matter of EU governance but also of domestic governance.

Article 11 TEU contains various provisions which complement the representative system:

1. The institutions shall, by appropriate means, give citizens and representative associations the opportunity to make known and publicly exchange their views in all areas of Union action.
2. The institutions shall maintain an open, transparent and regular dialogue with representative associations and civil society.
3. The European Commission shall carry out broad consultations with parties concerned in order to ensure that the Union's actions are coherent and transparent.
4. Not less than one million citizens who are nationals of a significant number of Member States may take the initiative of inviting the European Commission, within the framework of its powers, to submit any appropriate proposal on matters where citizens consider that a legal act of the Union is required for the purpose of implementing the Treaties.
    The procedures and conditions required for such a citizens' initiative shall be determined in accordance with the first paragraph of Article 24 of the Treaty on the Functioning of the European Union.

Article 12 sets out how national parliaments contribute to the "good functioning of the Union":

(a) through being informed by the institutions of the Union and having draft legislative acts of the Union forwarded to them in accordance with the Protocol on the role of national Parliaments in the European Union;
(b) by seeing to it that the principle of subsidiarity is respected in accordance with the procedures provided for in the Protocol on the application of the principles of subsidiarity and proportionality;
(c) by taking part, within the framework of the area of freedom, security and justice, in the evaluation mechanisms for the implementation of the Union policies in that area, in accordance with Article 70 of the Treaty on the Functioning of the European Union, and through being involved in the political monitoring of Europol and the evaluation of Eurojust's activities in accordance with Articles 88 and 85 of that Treaty;
(d) by taking part in the revision procedures of the Treaties, in accordance with Article 48 of this Treaty;
(e) by being notified of applications for accession to the Union, in accordance with Article 49 of this Treaty;
(f) by taking part in the inter-parliamentary cooperation between national Parliaments and with the European Parliament, in accordance with the Protocol on the role of national Parliaments in the European Union.[56]

Furthermore, the preamble to the EU's Charter of Fundamental Rights states that the EU is "founded on the principles of liberty, democracy, respect for human rights and fundamental freedoms, and the rule of law". These are core principles and the individual, rights and duties, are at the centre of the EU's activities.[57]

The EU Treaties provide mechanisms for national parliaments to contribute to the decision- making process. Under two legally binding protocols attached to the EU Treaties, national parliaments not only scrutinise EU documentation, but may object to Commission proposals. The *Protocol on the Application of the Principles of Subsidiarity and Proportionality* (the subsidiarity Protocol) sets out procedures for challenging draft legislation on the grounds of subsidiarity.[58] The *Protocol on the Role of National Parliaments* places obligations on EU institutions to send all documents to national parliaments and to wait up to eight weeks before adopting legislation so that they can effectively scrutinise the documentation and hold their governments to account with regard to them.[59] Article 9 of this Protocol also states that the EP and national parliaments "shall together determine the organisation and promotion of effective and regular interparliamentary cooperation within the Union".

The European Union: A Democratic Institution? 71

Under Article 5(3) TEU national parliaments "ensure compliance with the principle of subsidiarity in accordance with the procedure provides for in the Protocol" and in Article 12(b) TEU they "contribute actively to the good functioning of the Union" by seeing to it "that the principle of subsidiarity is respected". The second recital of the *Protocol on the Role of National Parliaments* recalls that Member States wish: "to encourage greater involvement of national Parliaments in the activities of the European Union and to enhance their ability to express their views on draft legislative acts as well as on other matters which may be of particular interest to them".

But did the Lisbon Treaty really fully involve national parliaments in European decision - making,[60] or did Lisbon merely give "the appearance of greater democratic legitimacy" to EU affairs?[61]

2.3. The 'Democratic Deficit'

A democratic deficit is said to exist where institutions fall short of general principles of democracy (e.g. participation, competition for power, election of political leadership by universal suffrage, transparency and accountability).

> EU definition (*Europa*) of democratic deficit:
>
> "The democratic deficit is a concept invoked principally in the argument that the European Union and its various bodies suffer from a lack of democracy and seem inaccessible to the ordinary citizen because their method of operating is so complex".

The guarantees of a representative democratic system have been formalised in the EU Treaties and have been confirmed by the Court of Justice of the EU (CJEU) on various occasions. The Treaties appear to provide a clear and equitable legal and constitutional basis for power, accountability and legitimacy, one that was negotiated and agreed by the leaders of all EU Member States and endorsed by their parliaments and/or electorates.

So why do so many accuse the EU of not being democratic, of having a 'democratic deficit'? The accompanying reading list to this paper contains a fraction of the literature on the subject of the EU's democratic deficit,[62] which has been a criticism of the EU from its very early days.

The term 'democratic deficit' in relation to the EU has been attributed to various originators. The German newspaper editor and intellectual Theo

Sommer referred to it in 1973.[63] The term was also used by the Young European Federalists in their 1977 manifesto and by the academic and former Labour MP David Marquand in 1979.[64] Although it emerged in the early 1970s, the democratic deficit has been attributed largely to successive EU Treaty amendments since 1986 (the *Single European Act*) which have incrementally reduced the powers of individual Member States and challenged the traditional concept of national sovereignty. The main characteristics are:

- The increased use of qualified majority voting (QMV – about 74%) for the adoption of legislation in the Council;
- Limiting Member States' powers by removing their veto in the Council of Ministers;
- Expanding the policy areas in which the EU has a role, sometimes excluding any
- action by Member States (EU 'exclusive competence');
- An increase in executive power and a decrease in national parliamentary control with deeper EU integration.

The following observations refer to other aspects of the perceived democratic deficit:[65]

- The EU's executive, the Commission, is unelected;
- The EP is too weak compared with the Council and Commission;
- EP elections are not really 'European' elections and turnouts are low;
- The EU is too distant from voters;
- The EU adopts policies that are not supported by a majority of EU citizens;
- The Court of Justice makes law rather than interpreting it;
- There is a lack of transparency in the Council's adoption of legislation and in certain appointments (e.g. EU Commissioners);
- EU law has primacy over national law and constitutions.

The EU and the Member States agree that the EU needs to tackle legitimacy issues, but they diverge over where the source of EU democratic legitimacy should lie. Several EU governments believe they should have more power, that the EU should be more inter- governmental. Some governments maintain that only their own national parliaments can make the EU more accountable and legitimate. They argue that the EU adopts decisions in which national parliaments have had only limited input and influence, that subsidiarity has been an ambiguous and elusive concept. Not until the Lisbon Treaty has there been a mechanism for involving national parliaments in alerting the Commission to subsidiarity issues through an 'Early Warning Mechanism' ('yellow card'), but this mechanism has been criticised for not compelling the Commission to rethink a proposal to which national parliaments object on subsidiarity grounds.[66] In evidence to the Lords EU Committee Inquiry into the Role of National Parliaments in the EU, Professor Dr Hermann-Josef Blanke, University of Erfurt, referred to this situation as a "paradox … in relation to the democratic principle, which the role of national Parliaments has been structured to foster". Furthermore, as MEP Andrew Duff has pointed out, while national parliaments thought that triggering a yellow card was a triumph for them and for democracy, the EP saw this as a failure of the democratic process.[67] Another development, the increased use of trilogues[68] and first reading agreements,[69] present legitimacy challenges to parliamentary scrutiny committees across the EU.

Some argue that a fundamental lack of understanding of the EP and the consequent lack of engagement between the EP and national parliaments contributes to the lack of democratic legitimacy of the EU as a whole and the EP in particular.

2.4. National Sovereignty and the Primacy of EU Law

As noted in section 1, sovereignty is about where and with whom power resides. Power is often expressed as 'competence' in the EU. The effects of the EU Treaties and EU law on national legislatures, the 'Europeanisation' of national law-making and the concept of 'pooled sovereignty' have all been problematic from time to time and have produced a body of case law at the CJEU – though not always in the national courts - that confirms the supremacy of EU law in the legal order of the Member States. Many international treaties require the pooling, and thus a limitation, of national sovereignty. This limitation arises, for example, from collective decision-making, majority voting, adherence to a particular set of rules or the obligation to bring national laws into line with a ratified treaty. Some have their own courts and monitoring mechanisms.[70]

Under customary international law, international treaties take precedence over domestic law where there is a conflict. The EU is no exception to this principle, but the EU is unique in having created its own legal system in which European laws are enacted as domestic laws. EU Regulations are directly applicable in all Member States, while directives and decisions are implemented as domestic laws. All are binding instruments. From the birth of the European Coal and Steel Community (ECSC) in 1951 and the European Economic Community (EEC) in 1957, Member States have been required to pool sovereignty in areas covered by the relevant Treaties, and the presumption has always been that EU membership is conditional upon a limitation of sovereignty. During the Second Reading of the *European Communities Bill* in 1972 the then Chancellor of the Duchy of Lancaster, Geoffrey Rippon, said of the provision which became section 2(2) of the *European Communities Act 1972* (the ECA):

> As for the future, our obligations will result in a continuing need to change the law to comply with non-direct provisions, and to supplement directly applicable provisions, and it is not possible in advance to specify the subjects which will have to be covered.[71]

As Paul Craig[72] points out, if a democratic Parliament agrees to EU membership, it also agrees to "some loss of autonomy", which is "characteristic of any collective action".[73] Not to do so could lead to a situation where EU membership would be untenable. Sir Konran Schiemann, former UK judge at the CJEU thinks it is "obvious that agreements from which anyone can escape at any time are pretty well useless".[74] On the other hand, as Roger Liddle points out in The Europe Dilemma: Britain and the Drama of EU Integration (2014), the concept of sovereignty pooling, which "succeeded brilliantly in bringing about reconciliation and an end to war on the European continent", has a quite different rationale today. The "simple test to which supranational sovereignty pooling should be subject" today, he argues, is whether "a case [can] convincingly be made that the national states of the EU will achieve significantly more through any new measure of sovereignty pooling than they could achieve on their own – in other words by the test of whether it delivers results".

Member States' constitutions provide for the transfer of sovereign powers to the EU or the pooling of sovereignty within the EU.[75] In the UK this has been achieved by means of the ECA. The UK Government was aware of the consequences of membership for national and parliamentary sovereignty long before the UK joined the EEC. They were drawn to the attention of the then Lord Privy Seal, Edward Heath, by the Lord Chancellor, Lord Kilmuir, who had no doubt that in signing the Treaty of Rome "we shall suffer some loss of sovereignty", but that "At the end of the day, the issue whether or not to join

.... must be decided on broad political grounds ...".[76] The ECA allowed the Government to confer competence on the EC/EU, and subsequent conferrals or extensions of competence have been authorised by amendments to this Act. Under Section 2(1) ECA all directly effective E U law is enforceable in the UK domestic courts. If the UK were to enact legislation which it knew contradicted EU law, the UK courts would be faced with a contradiction. In the UK one of the main exponents of the primacy issue was the so-called 'Metric Martyrs' case, *Thoburn v Sunderland City Council*.[77] In the appeal judgment, Lord Justice Laws confirmed the sovereignty of Parliament and Parliament's legislative supremacy vis-à-vis the EC, but thought the traditional doctrine had been modified, by the common law and "wholly consistently with constitutional principle".[78] He described how the Courts had found their way through the "*impasse* seemingly created by two supremacies, the supremacy of European law and the supremacy of Parliament", comparing the ECA to the "family" of "constitutional statutes" such as the *Magna Carta*, the *Bill of Rights*, the *Human Rights Act* and others.[79]

The doctrine of direct effect[80] and the primacy of EC/EU law[81] have been established by the CJEU. Lisbon Treaty Declaration 17 recalls ECJ case law in this respect and cites the *Opinion of the Council Legal Service* that "primacy of EC law is a cornerstone principle of Community law". EU law also has priority over other international law.[82] However, the primacy assumption continues to raise questions about sovereignty and whether, or to what extent, sovereignty can be limited or divided. Not all Member States have accepted the precedence of international law, claiming ultimate authority over potential infringements of their constitution by acts of international or EU law.[83]. Legal opinion is increasingly questioning the unconditional supremacy of international and EU law over domestic constitutional law, particularly where there is a conflict with core domestic values. According to Armin von Bogdandy,[84] "given the state of development of international law, there should be the possibility, at least in liberal democracies, of placing legal limits on the effect of a norm or an act under international law within the domestic legal order if it severely conflicts with constitutional principles".[85] In the view of Professor Anne Peters,[86] competing international and national laws need some kind of compromise mechanism based on respect for the democratic credentials of states:

> The task ahead then is to devise novel procedural mechanisms for the adjustment of competing claims of authority in order to realize what Mireille Delmas-Marty has called a 'pluralisme ordonné'.[142] For instance, it must be

acknowledged that national courts are under a *bona fide* obligation to take into account international law, must interpret domestic constitutional law as far as possible consistently with international prescriptions, and must give reasons for non-compliance. Moreover, any refusal to apply international law based on domestic constitutional arguments must be strictly limited to constitutional core values, and may be permissible only 'as long as' the constitutional *desiderata* have not been even in a rudimentary fashion incorporated into international law itself.[143] On the other hand, the international bodies should grant a margin of appreciation to national decision-makers with a strong democratic legitimation.[144] Of course these suggestions bear the real risk of reinforcing the perception that international law is only soft law or even no law at all, with little potential to place robust constraints on the exercise of political powers. They may therefore seem minimalist or even subversive for international law and global governance. However, it is my hope that procedural principles for ordered pluralism might work constructively, and provide, together with further democratization of international law, a flexible and sustainable response to counter nationalist tendencies and non-compliance with international law.[87]

Footnotes

[142] Mireille Delmas-Marty, Le pluralisme ordonné (Seuil Paris 2006).

[143] Cf German Constitutional Court, BVerfGE 37, 271 (1974) – Solange I.

[144] ECHR, *Hatton v. UK*, appl. No 36022/97, judgment of 8 July 2003, para. 97: 'The national authorities have a direct democratic legitimation and are, as the Court has held on many occasions, in principle better placed than an international court to evaluate local needs and conditions.'

Is "ordered pluralism" the answer to the sovereignty question for EU Member Sta tes? Can EU States be relied upon to devise, implement and sustain, even in the face of international turmoil, a democratic, legitimate and accountable system by which to be collectively governed? All 28 EU Member States are considered to be "free";[88] all are representative parliamentary democracies of one form or another and most have elected unicameral or bi - cameral legislatures.[89] This does not mean the EU system is automatically democratic, because the EU does not function as the sum of its component parts, but it probably means that the EU system stands a greater chance of being democratic than it would if its membership were largely dictatorships.

Fundamental contradictions remain as to how international treaty obligations sit with national sovereignty. Professor Mattias Kumm[90] has proposed that international law is inherently undemocratic, but that this might be mitigated if there is a strong link between international law and state consent:

But even then there is a residual problem, because many international obligations can't be unilaterally revoked by the state as a matter of international law, even when the majority of citizens using democratic procedures wants to do so. Problems of democratic legitimacy become even more serious, when Treaties authorize international institutions to make important social and political choices. Even if ultimately problem-solving or cooperation-enhancing benefits associated with international law may legitimate international law, there remains an aura of a legitimacy deficit that hangs over international law.[91]

The following section looks at the extent to which state (including parliamentary) consent contributes to the EU decision-making and institutional systems.

3. INSTITUTIONAL ISSUES

The democratic deficit is said to lie mainly in the structure, composition, powers, procedures and interaction of the main EU institutions, the Commission, Council, European Parliament (EP) and Court of Justice. In the institutional triangle that forms the EU's decision -making mechanism, the Commission proposes legislation while the EP and the Council debate and adopt it. This structure, which underpins the so-called 'Community method', was set up by the *Treaty of Rome* and has not changed fundamentally, although the EP has gained powers incrementally with each EU Treaty change. The European Council of Heads of State and government, although not a legislator, has, with the introduction of the post of president in 2009, gained considerable weight as the main provider of political leadership at EU level. The Commission's role and powers are largely unchanged since 1957. Its right to initiate legislation has survived Treaty amendments, although Paolo Ponzano *et al* have argued that "its exercise in practice has been progressively eroded by the expansion and normalization of the codecision procedure",[92] which involves the Council and EP in a complicated and lengthy process of debate and amendment (see below).

It was originally envisaged in the post-World War II context that the EEC's institutional structure would protect the interests of 'small' countries (then the three Benelux countries) and avoid the common weaknesses of intergovernmental institutions, such as the 'unanimity trap', which can delay or prevent decisions being adopted.[93] This concept has generally prevailed and the Commission's Governance White Paper in 2001 outlined the benefits of the 'Community method':

> The Community method guarantees both the diversity and effectiveness of the Union. It ensures the fair treatment of all Member States from the largest to the smallest. It provides a means to arbitrate between different interests by passing them through two successive filters: the general interest at the level of the Commission; and democratic representation, European and national, at the level of the Council and European Parliament, together the Union's legislature.

- The European Commission alone makes legislative and policy proposals. Its independence strengthens its ability to execute policy, act as the guardian of the Treaty and represent the Community in international negotiations.
- Legislative and budgetary acts are adopted by the Council of Ministers (representing Member States) and the European Parliament (representing citizens). The use of qualified majority voting in the Council is an essential element in ensuring the effectiveness of this method. Execution of policy is entrusted to the Commission and national authorities.
- The European Court of Justice guarantees respect for the rule of law.[94]

But critics have found the structure undemocratic. Professor Ian Ward commented that it did "not fit neatly" into the early definitions of democracy because it did not "respect the essential principle which lies at the heart of this constitutional tradition, the separation, and the balance, of powers.[95] Sonia Piedrafita commented on the singular nature of the EU's political system:

> ... the EU's political system largely differs from the system of separation of powers in place in modern democracies. The executive, legislative and judicial powers are not wielded exclusively by any single EU institution, and the checks and balances are understood in a different fashion. The principle of institutional balance – rather than Montesquieu's principle of separation of powers, which is overseen by the Court of Justice – ensures that EU institutions act within the limits of the powers conferred to them by the treaties. As for the principle of representation, the current distribution of seats of the European Parliament among member states represents a substantial deviation from equality, with the larger member states being underrepresented and the smaller states being largely overrepresented.2 Moreover, the legislative powers of the European Parliament are more limited than those of the national parliaments, and the EU executive branch does not depend on a majority in the European Parliament. Therefore, unlike

in liberal democracies, EU decisions do not necessarily reflect the 'will of the majority'.[96]

The EU does not have a government or president that citizens can vote out, and the political scientist, Peter Mair, has commented on the weaknesses of the EU system in not providing an effective opposition:

> ... it is clear that the EU misses the third great milestone that has marked the path to democratic institutions in the nation-states. That is, we are afforded a right to participate at the European level, even if we may now choose to avail ourselves of that right less frequently; and we are afforded the right to be represented in Europe, even if it is sometimes difficult to work out when and how this representative link functions; but we are not afforded the right to organize opposition within the European polity. There is no government– opposition nexus at this level. Second, and again following Dahl, as well as Kirchheimer and Schapiro, we know that a failure to allow for opposition within the polity is likely to lead either (a) to the elimination of opposition, and to more or less total submission; or (b) to the mobilization of an opposition of principle against the polity – to anti-European opposition and to Euroscepticism. Third, this development is also beginning to reach down into the domestic sphere, in that the growing weight of the EU, and its indirect impact on national politics, also helps to foster domestic democratic deficits, and hence also limits the scope for classical opposition at the national level. Here too, then, we might expect to see either the elimination of opposition or the mobilization of a new – perhaps populist – opposition of principle".[97]

3.1. European Commission

The Commission is widely seen as the most undemocratic of the EU's institutions. Its members cannot be put in place or removed directly by the ballot box. Its main source of legitimacy is said to lie with the vote of approval from the EP, together with the EP's power to dismiss the whole body, but this in turn raises questions about the legitimacy of the EP (see below). The Commission's executive powers of initiative and implementation also raise concerns. Since 1986 single market legislation has broadened the Commission's powers to propose legislation and to develop implementing rules, usually in the form of EU regulations.

> The Commission, the EU's 'executive', is a collegiate body composed of one Commissioner per Member State, "chosen on the ground of their general competence and European commitment from persons whose independence is beyond doubt" (Article 17(3) TEU).
>
> The Commission proposes and initiates legislation and monitors Member States' compliance with EU law and the Treaties. It represents the EU externally, promotes the general interests of the EU and mediates in its internal affairs. It also plays a major role in the allocation of large amounts of funding from the EU budget, such as agricultural subsidies and structural funds.
>
> Commissioners are nominated by Member States and are usually former politicians of high standing (e.g. former government ministers, even prime ministers). They are appointed by the Council by a qualified majority vote and with the consent of the EP. The Commission President is proposed by the European Council by QMV and elected by the EP by a majority of its members.

The Commission is not a 'party government' like a national government, and as no party holds power in the EU, no party is responsible for its policies. Analysts have also found that in EP elections people vote largely to express an opinion on what their national governments are doing, rather than what the Commission is doing. When during the Convention on the Future of Europe in 2001 several Member States suggested allowing the majority in the EP, instead of the European Council, to nominate the Commission President, there were objections from a minority of governments, including the UK and France, which feared this would be too 'federalist'. However, under the Lisbon Treaty reforms, the EP "elects", rather than approves the Council's proposed candidate for President (Article 7(7) TEU). The European Council must now also take into account the results of the most recent EP elections when proposing a candidate for the Commission presidency. The changes represent a degree of politicisation which many argue gives the EU as a whole more legitimacy.

Moves to Democratise the Commission

In 2013 the Commission President, José Manuel Barroso, in the Blueprint for a deep genuine economic and monetary union: Launching a European Debate,[98] maintained that democratic accountability can only be ensured at the level at which the executive decision is taken, while taking due account of the level at which the decision has an impact. The *Blueprint* called for greater

The European Union: A Democratic Institution? 81

involvement by national parliaments and the EP where there is further deepening of economic and monetary union, better EP and national scrutiny and greater inter-parliamentary cooperation between national parliaments and the EP (see also Section 4.3 on the euro crisis and Section 5 on dealing with the democratic deficit). The Commission has also initiated an EU-wide debate on the future of Europe by means of events, 'citizens' dialogues', internet polls and contributions to discussions.[99]

In an analysis of the Commission, Andreas Fischer-Hotzel[100] summarises recent innovations that aim to improve citizens' participation in Commission initiatives, citing the deliberative poll on 'Tomorrow's Europe', Citizens' Consultations,[101] multi-media websites (e.g. Twitter) and online forums such as 'Debate Europe': "These, and other projects, resonate with the European Union's strategy to strengthen democratic participation, demonstrated for example by the introduction of the principle of participatory democracy in the Treaty of Lisbon ".[102] But Fischer-Hotzel concludes that the Commission's attempts at participatory democracy fall short at a practical level because the EU does not have decision -making structures into which such contributions can be fed or acted upon:

> The application of participatory procedures in the EU representative democratic political system is faced with certain practical problems stemming from legal restrictions and the multi-level and multi-lingual nature of the Union. The Commission's approach to participation has been to run or sponsor selected projects which encourage citizens to engage in discussion and consultation, especially in the period from 2005 to 2007. These projects, however, fell short of the normative ideal of participation because they were not connected to a specific decision-making process and because the citizens' input was often mediated by civil society organisations. In addition, there is no evidence that decision-makers felt normatively bound by the results.
>
> Even the practical objective of discussion and (very general, unspecific) consultation could not be met satisfactorily for three reasons. First, face-to-face projects, which can necessarily involve only a limited number of people, were very few given the overall EU population of 500 million inhabitants, and online based projects could not attract great numbers of participants either, despite their technical potential. Second, not all instruments had a truly European dimension and some were confined to the local or regional level only. Third, all projects were faced with the problem of language. Only some projects provided adequate translation, but only at the price of a limited number of participants. Translation is costly, but no translation is exclusive. All these problems seem to be structural rather than accidental.

The author is doubtful as to whether future Treaty revision would be more receptive to participatory democracy, given the size and diversity of the EU and the range of interested parties that could potentially feed into policy- and decision-making. The use of the internet for participating in EU consultations, while valuable, is also criticised for not allowing participation in formal negotiations.

In the balance between participation by citizens/civil society and efficiency, the latter has been the priority, arguably in the interest of furthering EU integration. Some accuse the Commission of focusing on narrow economic interests over general public interest and a diverse range of civil society input. As Dr Femke van Esche[103] observes, this is a classic governance problem:

> ... the crux of politics at every level, local, national and European alike. The matter of achieving that delicate balance of fundamental, though not necessarily compatible values, such as democracy and efficiency, equality and autonomy. The classic problem of public administration: What degree of centralisation of power is required in order to act effectively, and how many checks and balances to vouch for sufficient public support?[104]

3.2. European Parliament

The European Parliament, directly elected since 1979, has for many years been the focus of arguments about the EU's democratic legitimacy. The premise was that if the EP were given more substantive legislative power to carry out the tasks of a real legislative assembly, the EU as a whole would become more accountable and the democratic deficit would be reduced. The EP has gained substantial power since the 1970s, with reform of the rules for adopting the EU's annual budget, which gave it a power of veto ove r "non-compulsory expenditure" (economic and social spending) and with direct elections and co -decision (now the Ordinary Legislative Procedure - OLP).[105]

From Assembly of National Politicians to Directly Elected Parliament

The European Assembly which pre-dated the EP was composed of national parliamentarians from the then nine Member States. It was largely deliberative but from the start was regarded as a precursor to a future, directly elected assembly. Yet, as early as 1955 there were doubts about a directly elected assembly: the Belgian Socialist MP, Pierre Wigny, said in a debate in the Coal and Steel Community Common Assembly on 24 June 1955 that a

The European Union: A Democratic Institution? 83

directly elected European assembly would "not create a shared sense of belonging among voters and would cut the valuable ties between the Assembly and national parliaments".[106] He elaborated:

> "The nature of European elections as second-order national elections is an indication not only of the dominance of national parties over European parties, but also of the attachment of national electorates to domestic politics".
>
> Stephen George and Ian Bache, Politics in the European Union, 2001

If there are no longer personal ties between national parliaments and ourselves; if there is a different mode of suffrage and different results of representation, such that we argue over the representative value, within the nations themselves, of such-and-such an Assembly; if, this unity having been achieved, the Chambers are not re-elected at the same time and the vote of one side can be considered by the other side as involving a necessary change in government, then I fear that, through these highly premature reforms, which try to do too much too soon by endeavouring to guarantee a democratic nature which, I repeat, is indispensable, but already largely accomplished, we will arouse the fears of those who worry about the colossal shadow of a hypothetical Europe which would efface the various differences which exist and which must continue to exist between historic states and ancient nations.[107]

The 1972 Vedel Report, 'Growth of Competency in the European Parliament', argued for the EEC's "Community element" to be reinforced. The report was optimistic that the Parliament could move towards a single electoral law once it had gained legitimacy on the strength of its first direct election. From 1979 directly elected MEPs sat in pan-European political groups (Socialist, Conservative, Liberal, Green etc) and not in national delegations. The Spanish MEP, Miguel Angel Martínez, giving evidence to the Lords EU Committee inquiry into the Role of National Parliaments in the EU, described a situation in the EP which reflected what he described as a "deficiency" both at national and EU level: that political majorities in the Council and EP make decision-making predictable and inevitable:

What I feel to be a deficiency in the process, in terms of the democratic functioning of all of our societies as well as these institutions, is that the same political majority that exists in the Council is the same political majority that exists in the European Parliament. What that means—and this is a larger scale of what happens in many member states, and it happened for a long time in my country—is that the European Parliament, despite having this role of exercising democratic scrutiny over the executive body, is dominated by the same political majority. That is what is happening here now. Very often, even though the Parliament has co-decision powers, because we have the same political majority in Parliament as we do in Council, the proposals that Council comes out with end up being imposed. That limits the ability of the European Parliament to amend the proposals and the effect is lessened. I do not think that is satisfactory and that is something that could be improved in terms of the way the Parliament works.[108]

The belief was that the directly elected assembly would be more democratic and therefore more legitimate in the eyes of the EU electorate. But could the former Assembly of elected national politicians have been a more democratic institution? In an article in 2010 Anand Menon[109] and John Peet[110] thought the 1979 EP elections had indeed broken the direct link between national parliaments and the EP, and that direct elections had "come at a cost in lost legitimacy at home":

> The model of the European Assembly [...] solved this problem by choosing delegates from national parliaments as MEPs. But after direct elections were introduced in 1979, this organic link with national parliaments was weakened and, when dual mandates (allowing MEPs simultaneously to serve as MPs in their own country) were scrapped, later broken altogether.[111]

Could the EP return to its former composition of national parliamentarians? The increased use of co-decision, which involves the EP at all stages of the decision-making process, and the expansion of policy areas in which the EU acts, mean that an MEP's workload is much heavier today than it was in the 1950s, 60s and 70s, when the Assembly had virtually no legislative powers.[112] As Menon and Peet point out, this would probably make such an assembly untenable today; they argue instead for finding a better way of involving national parliaments in EU decision-making, and suggestions as to how this could be done are discussed in Section 5.3).

EP Gains in Legislative Powers

Since 1986 the Member States have agreed through Treaty changes to give the EP more legislative power:

- The *Single European Act* of 1986 helped redress the institutional balance by giving the EP a second reading. Under the 'cooperation procedure', the Council could only approve a previously rejected proposal by a unanimous vote rather than by a qualified majority. Also, the EP received the right to veto the accession of new Member States and assent with the Council to international agreements.
- The Maastricht Treaty introduced co-decision and gave the EP an ultimate right to veto a legislative proposal by an absolute majority after two readings of the Council and EP.
- The Amsterdam and Nice Treaties extended the use of co-decision, giving the EP a say in a wider range of matters. The Nice Treaty gave the EP the right to institute proceedings before the ECJ seeking to review acts of the institutions
- The Lisbon Treaty made co-decision (renamed the Ordinary Legislative Procedure - OLP) the EU's default decision-making procedure and extended it to justice and home affairs areas such as immigration, offences and penalties, police cooperation and aspects of trade and agriculture policy. The EP gained almost equal rights with the Council in the adoption of legislation.
- Lisbon abolished the distinction between 'compulsory' and 'non-compulsory' expenditure, so that now the EP and Council determine all EU expenditure together.

The EP has also 'democratised' through soft powers, such as its right, by a two -thirds majority, to pass a motion of censure against the Commission, to question the Commission and Council at a regular question time and establish committees of inquiry to in vestigate cases of poor administration by the EU institutions. In spite of these gains, the EP's relative weakness compared with the Council and Commission, and the repeatedly low turnout for EP elections, tend to support assertions that the directly elected and more powerful EP does not remedy the EU's democratic deficit. As Dr Julie Smith, Cambridge University, told the Lords EU Committee inquiry:

> Granting the EP more powers only responded to one element of the democratic deficit, however. It ensured that there was a parliamentary dimension to legislative and budgetary decisions within the EU but it did not tackle the problems associated with holding national ministers to account for their actions within the Council of the EU. This was, and remains, primarily a task for national parliaments. How well national parliaments are able to fulfil

this role depends in part on the formal powers of NPs under the Treaties but also on political will and resources within the various national chambers

For some, the EP is part of the legitimacy problem. Professor Adam Cygan, University of Leicester, in written evidence to the Lords Inquiry on the Role of National Parliaments in the EU, thought that "unlike national parliaments which are expressions of popular democracy in each Member State, the European Parliament does not share many of the democratic credentials of national parliaments, remains distant from citizens and within the process of EU decision-making may be viewed as part of the legitimacy problem". Roger Godino and Fabien Verdier thought that although the EP is "the sole democratic element in the whole fabric, [it] is seen as a hotbed of lobbying rather than as a shrine of democracy, and its members are elected on lists organised by political parties and consisting primarily of those politicians who fail to win the support of their own countries' electorates" (to which their answer is the creation of a European democratic federation).[113] Some are even more sceptical: Charles Grant of the Centre for European Reform (CER) suggests that "Much of the time, the parliament's priority appears to be more power for itself ... The parliament always wants 'more Europe' - a bigger budget and a larger role for the EU".[114]

Many commentators and would-be reformers emphasise the importance of the forthcoming EP elections as a chance for EU citizens to shape the EU for the next five years: Commissioner Viviane Reding said on 7 January 2014 that the elections were "Europe's democratic moment. We must make sure citizens seize it" She appealed to voters to participate and not shun the ballot box or vote in protest for eurosceptic parties. In his speech at the opening ceremony of the Greek Presidency on 8 January 2014, President Barroso also called on EU citizens to contribute to the shaping of Europe by voting in the EP elections:

> The buck stops, and rightly so, at the political leaders' desk. But governments and institutions alone cannot tackle the complex challenges we face. That requires engaged European citizens. That is why we all should care about the upcoming European elections. It truly does cut to the heart of our European future and the unity of Europe.

But this kind of rhetoric has not worked in the past: EP elections have been too remote and 'foreign' for the vast majority of EU citizens; EU reform too intangible and the EU too incomprehensible.

The Turnout Problem[115]

In modern democracies election turnout is seen as a key measure of political engagement, with low or decreasing turnout often seen as an indicator of political disengagement or disenchantment. The OECD states: "High voter turnout is desirable in a democracy because it increases the chance that the political system reflects the will of a large number of individuals, and that the government enjoys a high degree of legitimacy".[116]

Figure 1 below shows that there has been a general decline in turnout since the first EP parliamentary election in 1979. This is true for the countries with the maximum (when excluding compulsory voting) and minimum voter turnouts, as well as average voter turnout across the years. The average turnout has fallen from 62% in 1979 to 43% in 2009. Even countries that have traditionally seen high turnout such as Italy have seen a decline (a fall of 20.6% in the same time period).[117] With the exception of the 1999 EP elections, UK-wide turnout in the EP elections has remained relatively steady since 1979, but is consistently among the lower turnouts in the EU.[118] In States with compulsory voting, such as Belgium and Luxembourg, turnout has been consistent and high.[119]

Is this trend also true of national elections? Using data from the Institute for Democracy and Electoral Assistance's (IDEA) Unified Database,[120] Figure 2 shows the average turnout at EU and national parliamentary elections in each of the 28 member states from 1989 to 2013. While there has been a progressive decline in turnout for both EP and national elections, the decline in EU turnout has been more pronounced. Between 1989 and 2009 turnout for EU elections fell by 15.4% compared with 11.6% in the case of national elections.

Turnout gaps (defined as the difference in voter turnouts between EU elections and the most recent national elections) show any differences within and between countries in terms of their preference to vote in national over EU elections. The average voter turnout gap for the 2009 EP election was 22.8% i.e. in the 2009 election, the average EU member stat e was likely to see a 22.8% lower turnout than in its most recent national election. The three countries with the largest and smallest turnout gaps are represented in figure 3, showing that while in almost all EU countries more people are likely to vote in national elections than EU ones, the scale of this difference varies significantly across the EU.

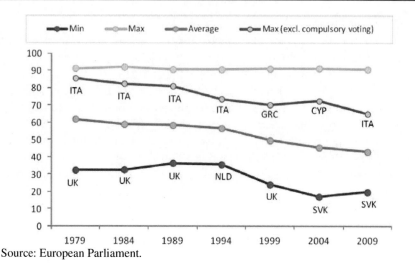

Source: European Parliament.

Figure 1. Maximum, minimum and average voter turnout at European Elections (1979-2009).

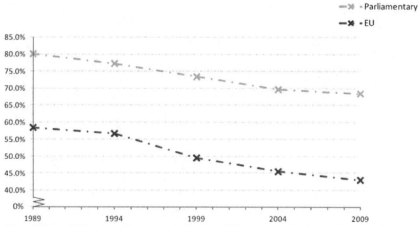

Note: Where EU and parliamentary elections did not occur in the same year, the most recent parliamentary election was used.

Figure 2. Average voter turnout at national parliamentary and EU elections, 1989-2009[121].

The European Union: A Democratic Institution? 89

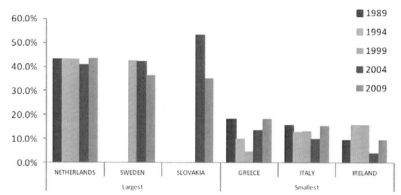

Note: Where EU and parliamentary elections did not occur in the same year, the most recent parliamentary election was used.

Figure 3. Largest and smallest voter turnout gaps between national and EU elections, 1989- 2009[122].

While the average difference in turnout between national and EU elections has increased from 17.5% in 1989 to 22.8% in 2009 (+5.3%), the gap has fallen slightly since peaking in 1999 (24.1%).

Why Do EU Citizens Not Vote in EP Elections?

Eurobarometer polls give an insight into reasons behind the fall in EU election turnout[123] in relation to satisfaction with EU democracy and attitudes towards EU membership.

Interest in EU Issues

Is there any link between the citizens of EU Member States' interest in EU issues and voter turnout? In figure 4, the left panel shows the proportion of those who responded to a poll about interest in EU issues by stating that they are "a great deal interested" (with each point on the graph representing high interest for a given country in a given year).[124] There appears to be a somewhat positive trend between being "a great deal interested" and voter turnout. The right panel represents the trend in the average proportion of those reporting to be "a great deal interested", showing a clear decline in interest in EU issues over time.

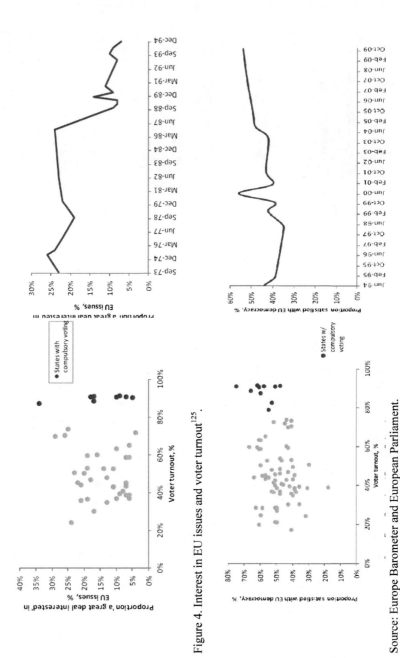

Figure 4. Interest in EU issues and voter turnout[125].

Figure 5. Satisfaction with EU democracy and voter turnout.

Source: Europe Barometer and European Parliament.

Satisfaction with EU Democracy

Another question was about satisfaction with EU democracy. Satisfaction here is defined as a response of either 'very satisfied' or 'fairly satisfied' in response to the poll.[126] In the left panel of figure 5 the scatter graph links the percentage of those who report being satisfied with EU democracy and the relationship of this percentage with voter turnout. Again, there appears to be a positive relationship, intuitively indicating that the more satisfied the population of a country is, the higher the turnout. However, the right-hand panel indicates that the average satisfaction with EU democracy across the EU has actually been going up in recent years. Given the left-hand panel, this would imply that voter turnouts should actually be *increasing*, suggesting that satisfaction with EU democracy is unlikely to be the underlying cause for low turnout.

Attitudes Towards EU Membership

What about the attitudes of citizens of EU countries towards their country's membership of the EU and how this relates to voter turnout?[127] Figure 6 shows that the decline in EU voter turnout since 1979 has coincided with the average proportion of people stating that EU membership is 'a good thing'. This may contribute towards an explanation for declining voter turnout. However, it should be noted that in recent years there appears to b e an uptick in the average proportion of positive attitudes towards EU membership.

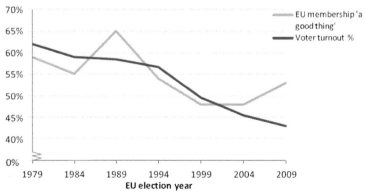

Source: Europe Barometer and European Parliament.

Figure 6. Average proportion of those with a positive attitude towards EU membership and voter turnout.

Figure 7 below also represents the average proportion of those rating EU membership 'a good thing', showing substantial differences among the different members of the EU, a gap that has been growing over time and may account for the widening gaps in voter turnout.

Trust in EU Institutions

In 2011, a year marked by the global financial crisis, *Standard Eurobarometer 76* reported a sharp decline in trust in the EU institutions and in national institutions. *Standard Eurobarometer 78* found in autumn 2012 that more European citizens considered the EU to be undemocratic than democratic. *Standard Eurobarometer* reported in July 2013:

> More than two-thirds of Europeans say that their voice does not count in the EU (67%), a 3-point increase taking this score to its highest level since autumn 2004 (EB62) when the question was first asked. This proportion has increased almost continuously since spring 2009 (EB71), from 53% up to 67%. Slightly more than a quarter of respondents (28%, - 3) agree that their voice counts in the EU.[...]
>
> In 24 EU Member States, absolute majorities of respondents disagree that their voice counts in the EU. This opinion is most widespread in Greece (89%) and Cyprus (89%), but is also very common in Portugal (81%), in Italy (78%) and in Spain (77%). These five countries in the south of the EU are joined by the Czech Republic (81%) and Estonia (77%).

In evidence to the Lords EU Committee inquiry, Dr Eleni Panagiotarea commented on the "political limits" in citizens' trust in national institutions when linked to support for the EU:

> Citizens may no longer be content with the performance of their respective parliamentary democracies in the EU framework and casting a vote may no longer suffice to give 'citizenship' a substantive meaning. Interestingly, the declining trend in citizens' trust in both the EU and national governments and parliaments, evident in successive Eurobarometer surveys and other surveys has not set the alarm bells ringing.

Analysing the Turnout Issues

Is the EU undemocratic because people do not vote? Do people not vote because the EU is undemocratic? A *Flash Eurobarometer* in March 2013 asked voters whether voting in EP elections was an effective way of influencing political decisions:

The European Union: A Democratic Institution?   93

54% think voting in EU elections is an effective means of influencing political decision-making. At least 50% of people in 19 Member States agree that voting in European elections is an effective way to influence political decisions. Romania (71%) has the highest number of people who take this view, followed by Malta (69%) and Italy (65%).

In four EU countries a majority of respondents think that voting in European elections is not an effective way to influence political decisions: Latvia (61%), the Czech Republic (54%), the UK (54%) and Slovenia (53%). Opinion is equally divided in the Netherlands, with 49% of respondents agreeing and 49% disagreeing that it is effective.[128]

Would an increase in votes for eurosceptic parties such as UKIP, Italy's *Five Star Movement* or Denmark's *People's Movement against the EU* indicate that the EU is democratic or undemocratic? The process is democratic but such an outcome would bolster the argument that the electorate does not believe in the EU as a democratic institution.

Analysts have found that voting in EP elections, as well as being low across the EU, tends to be based on domestic issues. These, Anand Menon argued in 2009, are rehearsed in a "confused" and "apathetic" way in EP elections:

> ... beyond the "operational" flaws in the way elections to the European parliament work, the indifference of many citizens has deeper roots. Most fundamentally, member-states retain control over all those areas of public policy that polls routinely show to be the primary concern of their electorates: health, welfare spending, education and direct taxation among them. It is little wonder, then, that "real" political debate occurs at national level; or that European elections are regarded as (in political-science jargon) as "second-order elections" in which electorates feel free to experiment. The European Union, in other words, is structurally condemned to elicit electoral apathy.[129]

Before the last EP elections in 2009, Julia De Clerck-Sachsse and Piotr Maciejkaczynski thought that politicising the debate in the EP might help halt the trend of low turnout:

> If growing powers are matched with continually falling turnout, the logic of strengthening the European Parliament's powers as a means of democratising EU governance is undermined. In order to halt this trend, the next European Parliament should therefore carefully balance the need for efficiency with its role as a public forum for political debate. Therefore, more efforts should be made to politicise the debate in the EP, and debate in

plenary should be structured around the most politically salient questions. Indeed, the experience of the Services Directive has shown that, while difficult, it is possible for the Parliament to shape controversial policy.

Moreover, in addition to making EU policy more relevant to the public, the EP elections should be personalised, presenting 'faces' that the public can recognise and relate to. In this regard the role of national parties is also crucial in presenting candidates to the EP that are able to make an impact and in giving some space to European themes in the European election campaign.[130]

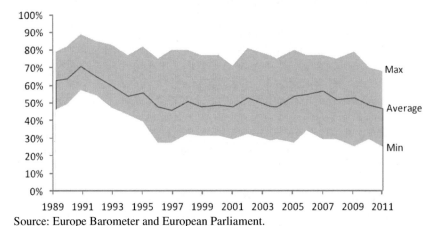

Source: Europe Barometer and European Parliament.

Figure 7. Average proportion of those with a positive attitude towards EU membership and voter turnout.

However, turnout in the 2009 EP elections reached a record average low of 43%.

According to a report by the US-based Pew Research Centre on a poll in March 2013 in eight EU Member States,[131] support for the EU is declining sharply, particularly in France, "suggesting that an economic crisis has become an existential crisis for the EU".[132] Positive views of the EU were only 41%, support for more integration had fallen to (below a third); young people were much less likely to view the EU positively than the population as a whole, except in Greece and Germany. There were some positive views in the Eurozone, where around two-thirds of respondents supported the continued use of the euro, and only the Greek and Polish voters wanted greater government spending rather than cuts. Germany was positive in most responses on economic, political and EU matters.

The European Union: A Democratic Institution?   95

Current public opinion polls generally show an increase in euroscepticism, with low levels of trust in the EU institutions and little support for further EU integration or enlargement. Tony Barber wrote in January 2014 that "Underlying everything is the frustration of Europeans that they exert less influence than ever over the decisions of elites, both in their own countries and in Brussels".[133] Attempts to bring the EU closer to its citizens, including through participatory opportunities, appear to be having little effect on the majority view that the EU, with its institutions, politicians and technocrats, lacks democratic legitimacy.

EP elections have been described as 'second-order elections' because of the lack of engagement of MEPs and the electorate with what could be described as a genuine political process. Ben Crum[134] wrote in 2003 that this "second-order character" of the EP elections also reflected upon its internal workings. "Although the Parliament is organised in cross- national ideological party groups, in day-to-day practice MEPs operate first of all from within their national political faction. Also most of their public engagement is oriented to their own national sphere".[135]

Peter Grand and Guido Tiemann[136] assessed data from a 2009 EP election survey, concluding that many EU citizens found EP elections insufficiently rewarding and that the perceived benefits of voting were often outweighed by the costs. "[T]here is 'less at stake' because no government emerges from the electoral process, the EP remains the weaker partner compared to the Council of Ministers in the legislative decision-making process and citizens do not feel "adequately represented by political parties in EP elections".[137] This conclusion supports the view that the EP is not the root of the legitimacy problem: it is not that the EP does not act democratically, but that it does not adequately represent the people in the EU. Christian Wohlfahrt[138] emphasised the German Constitutional Court's view (see Appendix) that EU citizens' right to vote is a "complementary possibility of participation in the system of European institutions",[139] and represents "complementary democratic legitimisation". It confirms the earlier German ruling on the Maastricht Treaty in this respect.[140]

The EP has many democratic credentials, as Menon has noted:

> To be clear: the European parliament is in many ways an admirable institution, populated by a number of hard-working, dedicated and highly able members (MEPs). Indeed, in those areas where it enjoys coequal status with the council of ministers in the legislative process, it is far more effective than virtually any parliament in any domestic setting. Its committees produce

enlightening and thoughtful reports; it has frequently shown itself able to amend and even veto legislation proposed by the commission and endorsed by the member-states in the European council.[141]

David Schleicher[142] has commented on the gap between the EP's democratic credentials and its actual effect:

> ... the EP looks and sounds like a democratically elected legislature, with parties organizing votes, predictable ideological splits, lobbyists loitering in the hallways, and members making preening speeches. Yet, there is one missing element: any semblance of democratic control. Voters have no idea who the MEPs are, do not care about what they do, and certainly do nothing to punish their bad behavior. Voter disengagement from the EP has ensured that the decision to give it more power failed to confer much democratic legitimacy on the EU as a whole. In fact, polls reveal a collapse in popular support for the EU since granting the EP real power.

He is puzzled by the lack of interest in the EP:

> With the ability to pass legislation that affects hundreds of millions of people in an increasing number of ways, the EP is now undoubtedly an important body— in last the last few years, they have passed legislation governing everything from carbon emissions to mobile telephony—and it is therefore both surprising and problematic that voters cannot be bothered to form independent judgments about its policies. It is equally surprising that despite the flaws of its elections, European states continue to grant the EP more power in an effort to resolve the democratic deficit, like a nervous gambler doubling his bets after a series of losses.[143]

But, in Menon's view, it lacks credibility as a democratic institution because EP elections "*do not work*- they fail to provide a parliament with a genuine mandate for action at European level". Menon confessed that it was "hard to imagine a sensible way in which to make them do so". Hix and Follesdal comment on the lack of opportunity for popular opinion to influence EU policy through a process of party political debate:

> A key difference between standard democratic and non-democratic regimes ... is that citizens form their views about which policy options they prefer through the processes of deliberation and party contestation that are essential elements of all democracies. Because voters' preferences are shaped by the democratic process, a democracy would almost definitely produce

The European Union: A Democratic Institution?

outcomes that are different to those produced by 'enlightened' technocrats. Hence, one problem for the EU is that its policy outcomes may not be those policies that would be preferred by a political majority after a debate.[144]

The Lisbon Treaty introduced new EP election procedures which will be used for the first time at the EP elections in May 2014. Electorates will not only elect MEPs, but also indirectly choose candidates for Commission President to replace José Manuel Barroso, whose term ends in 2014. The conduct of the EP elections was the subject of a Commission Communication and a Recommendation on enhancing the democratic and efficient conduct of the 2014 EP elections:[145] the European political parties would name their preferred candidates for the presidency and the chosen politician would then seek support in his/her own State. These recommendations, which are not legally binding, aim to make clearer the link between national and EP parties. The UK Government did not support them. David Lidington, Minister for Europe, said in an Explanatory Memorandum in April 2013 that "if national political parties wish to make their connection to European political parties known ... they are welcome to do so, but they should not be under any obligation in this regard". Overall, the Government was dismissive of the proposals, stating that they: "... appear to seek to assign more weight to the European Parliament's role than is provided for in the Treaties. Moreover, they argue that the basis for making such a change is to encourage an increase in electoral turnout. The documents provide no rationale for this assumption, other than a comparison with US electoral turnout ..." .

3.3. The Council of the EU

Council Secrecy and Moves Towards Openness

In the view of its critics the Council has always been secretive and its procedures opaque. Before the adoption in 2001 of a Regulation on transparency and access to documents, most Council documents were not publicly available and the Council's rules on confidentiality were incompatible with democratic standards. In 1995 Deidre Curtin summarised fears at that time about opening up Council meetings: "either progress would be blocked, because delegations would be forced to take up immoveable positions or the public proceedings would result in theatre, with the real business being done by officials behind closed doors".[146] Some of these fears have transpired, particularly with the increase in co-decision, which has meant more behind-the-scenes bargaining both by officials and government ministers.

> The intergovernmental Council of the EU comprises government ministers from a ll EU Member States and meets in sectoral formations to discuss and adopt legislation. The Council is the link between Member States and the EU.
>
> A 1992 Maastricht Treaty Declaration stated that "transparency of the decision-making process strengthens the democratic nature of the institutions and the public's confidence in the administration", and there were subsequent pledges from the Institutions in support of more openness and transparency in the Council.
>
> Critics believe that since Council decision-making by Qualified Majority Voting (QMV) was extended by the 1986 Single European Act in order to quickly adopt a large amount of internal market legislation, the EU has 'accumulated' a democratic deficit.
>
> The default voting procedure is now 'co-decision' with a qualified majority (around 74%) of the total number of votes required to adopt legislation. Analyses of voting behaviour in the Council tend to conclude that even where QMV is required, the Council prefers to reach a consensus. It does not vote formally in many cases where QMV is required, and much of the decision-making is believed to be done before proposals even reach the Council in the Committee of Permanent Representatives (COREPER) and Council working groups. Other factors may influence the outcome of a QMV decision, such as the preference of the Presidency, coalition forming, the 'shadow of the vote', informal bilateral contacts and 'horse-trading'.

In October 1993 the Council started to publish press releases detailing topics discussed and measures and common positions adopted, indicating which Member States voted against or had reservations. Later came the publication of timetables and agendas, a monthly summary of Council Acts, Council Minutes and the outcome of voting on legislative acts at Public Votes.[147] There has been a Public Register of Council documents since January 1999. Article 15 TFEU provides for public access to the documents of the EU institutions and openness in the decision-making process for draft legislative acts. The Council sits in public when it is discussing and voting on a proposal for a legislative act or when there is a general debate . Council minutes concerning the adoption of legal acts are published on the Council's

The European Union: A Democratic Institution? 99

Consilium website; access to other Council minutes can be requested. There are also live webcasts of public meetings on Consilium.

Critics maintain that although new rules of procedure have increased the Council's transparency, its processes are still opaque, which in turn affects the ability of national parliaments to effectively scrutinise its work.[148] EU and national civil servants do much of the negotiating before government ministers formally adopt a measure. Government ministers may eventually accept a compromise agreement which might not be popular with their parliament or the public. In such cases, ministers might exploit the lack of transparency to avoid taking responsibility for unpopular EU decisions. The EU Council does not often vote formally on matters where QMV is required. It prefers to continue negotiating until there is consensus in the Council. The QMV rules are still important because they help States to determine the likely outcome if a vote were held, but the lack of a formal vote makes it difficult to evaluate outcomes or to ascertain which States lined up where in the decision - making procedure. A lack of accountability is thus inherent in the Council's working procedures.

Sara Hagemann, co-author of a report by *Votewatch Europe,* believes the Council is now more transparent than many national legislatures, but Simon Hix, in evidence to the European Scrutiny Committee (ESC), argued that the Council was still too secretive and ought to make *everything* available to the public (Q431):

> ... when the Council is operating as a legislature, let us recognise it as a legislature. Let us have everything out in the open; let us have all the documents and all the position papers of all the Governments. Let us see up front what coalitions are formed between what Governments. They have to share speaking time, for example. They have to cosponsor amendments. Has this Government ever admitted to you who they cosponsor amendments with? I doubt it. Why not? They have to do it. With 27 member states and limited time, this is how they now organise the Council agenda, but we do not see any of that as citizens, and I think that is appalling.

He thought it was important that all Council negotiations – presumably including those in the Committee of Permanent Representatives (COREPER) and working groups - should be opened up (Q447):

> ... it would be more helpful for the legitimacy of the EU if this was transparent and we learnt that you win some and you lose some and this is part of the process. We could stick all this up online, we could look at it, we

could analyse it and we could see whether it is true that we lose more than other member states. We do not know that. Nobody knows that.

The Ordinary Legislative Procedure

The Lisbon Treaty made the OLP (co- decision) with QMV the general rule for EU decision-making.

The OLP involves up to three readings of a Commission proposal and co-legislative powers for the EP and Council. The OLP is lengthy, often with much to-ing and fro-ing between institutions,[149] but the Commission describes it as "the most legitimate from a democratic point of view".[150]

The scope of co-decision almost doubled under Lisbon, applying to 85 legal bases from 44 previously.[151] Unanimity is still required in 72 cases in the TFEU,[152] the main areas being taxation, social security and the accession of new States to the EU; and it remains the main decision-making procedure for foreign, security and defence policy in the TEU.

But as the EP has gained powers via co-decision, the national legislatures have lost them, and, as Anne Elisabeth Stie says, it cannot be taken for granted that making the EP a co- legislator with the Council will automatically make EU decision- making more democratic:

> Including the EP is not a guarantee in itself that the MEPs will behave democratically. We can also not simply assume that the ministers meeting in the Council can be conceived as channels where the views of affected parties (i.e. their respective national constituencies) are voiced. Moreover, the evaluative framework provides the conditions for showing when co-decision acts are satisfactorily subjected to democratic scrutiny and when unelected participants become too dominant and autonomous to be compatible with democratic decision-making.[153]

Steve Peers finds the OLP lacking in openness and transparency:

> The ordinary legislative procedure can be compared to the legislative process in any State with a bicameral legislature; its closest comparators are perhaps the legislative procedures in Germany (within the EU) and the United States (outside it). However, the legislative process in any democratic State compares favourably to that of the EU as far as openness and transparency is concerned.[154]

The European Union: A Democratic Institution?

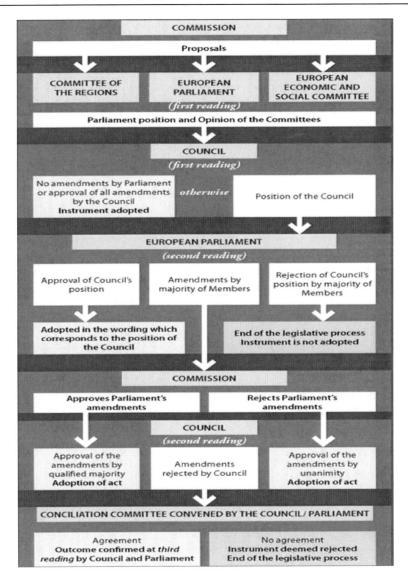

Its complexity and capacity to provide more opportunities for informal, behind-the-scenes agreement have hindered national parliamentary scrutiny - with implications for transparency and accountability both at EU and national levels. Bill Cash, Chair of the Commons European Scrutiny Committee, finds it undemocratic:

Through the ordinary legislative procedure, the United Kingdom has been assisting in the proliferation of informal meetings and early agreements. The ordinary legislative procedure with the inclusion of the trialogue meetings and the early agreements could not have been more undemocratic. It has consistently undermined the Westminster Parliament. Under this procedure it is increasingly difficult for Westminster to manage the way in which European Union affairs are conducted and how legislation is passed. The negotiations are informal so it is very difficult for national parliamentary committees to assemble information, and to decide speedily enough in order to have any impact on the final outcome of an early agreement dossier.[155]

Stie thinks that co-decision, in practice, is undemocratic:

> ... the democratic legitimacy of the co-decision procedure suffers from two main deficits: Firstly, the relationship between elected politicians and unelected experts is biased towards the latter in the sense that co-decision acts are to a large extent made by experts and bureaucrats. Secondly, the trialogues move the policy-making process behind closed doors where only a limited number of participants are present and of which only a half is elected politicians. In sum, the established practices of co-decision-making lead to a situation where politically and publicly salient issues are canalised into closed settings. A privatisation of politics has never been compatible with democratic decision- making.[156]

Peers suggests an Inter-institutional Agreement to remedy the lack of accountability in the OLP, which he outlines as follows:

> It provides for the prior adoption of a negotiating position by the EP and the Council – which must be publicly available – before first-reading negotiations start (points 1 to 3). This would confirm the developments in the EP, to the extent that committee mandates are becoming the norm, and would add a requirement of making the relevant documents available.
>
> Detailed information on all aspects of the negotiations must be available to the public (point 4). The final provisional text of any deal must in particular be public (point 5), and be widely publicised (in practice by means of press releases and updates on the dedicated website), in particular to national parliaments. There must then be at least eight weeks for national parliaments and civil society to scrutinise the final deal before any vote (based on the national parliaments' scrutiny period at the start of the legislative process) – although national parliaments could ask for an extension of this period (point 6).

For all this information to be accessible, there would be a single specialised website (point 7). At the moment, the separate 'co-decision' sites of the Commission, EP and Council are hard to find, contain much less information, and are infrequently updated. This site should be a broader forum for discussion of the proposals – including comments by civil society and interventions by national parliaments. There should be provision for interactivity, if, for instance, national ministers or MEPs want to respond to comments or to explain the latest developments.

Finally, since proposals to codify EU legislation do not make any substantive amendments to that legislation, there is no need to apply the rules to those proposals (point 9).

Qualified Majority Voting

Successive Treaty amendments have reduced the number of policy areas subject to unanimous voting in the Council, and the default voting procedure is now by a qualif ied majority (QM). Various informal arrangements have sought to mitigate any possible negative effects for individual Member States. In 1965 the so-called 'Luxembourg Compromise' (LC) added another dimension, outside the Treaty framework, in the form of an unofficial national veto. It was an agreement that where "very important interests of one or more partners" were at stake, ministers in the Council would try to reach unanimous solutions, even if the Treaty required only a majority. The UK Government was enthusiastic about the compromise, which seemed to be an instrument of democracy even though it stood outside the Treaties. It has been a somewhat fragile guarantee of national interests, however, and a pretty blunt instrument of democracy. The LC has rarely been invoked formally at ministerial level since the 1980s and increasingly the threat of majority voting has given way to a protracted search for consensus in the Council, although according to accounts of Council processes, it has been invoked informally on several occasions at sub-ministerial level (e.g. at the Committee of Permanent Representatives –COREPER).

The LC was never popular with the EU institutions because it had the potential to delay agreement on legislative proposals, just as the EU was trying to move away from national vetoes in the interests of completing the single market. Its use has undergone some refinement since its invention by de Gaulle as a totally unilateral national stance. It was to some extent supplanted by the 'Ioannina Compromise' of 1994, another 'gentlemen's agreement' that if a Member State government believed its vital interests were threatened by a proposal, but could not muster a blocking minority, the decision would be delayed while attempts to find a satisfactory solution were made. The Treaties now contain so-called "emergency brakes" in a number of areas which have the effect of stalling negotiations if important national interests are at stake. In addition, under the Protocol on subsidiarity and proportionality national parliaments are able to submit to the Commission a reasoned opinion on a proposal which they do not believe conforms with the principle of subsidiarity (this is discussed in more detail in Sections 2.2, 5.4 and 6.3). Not all would agree that the LC no longer exists, although it is true to say that its relevance has diminished over the last decade.

QUALIFIED MAJORITY VOTING

Since the accession of Croatia to the EU on 1 July 2013, when all 28 Member States are voting, a qualified majority (QM) is at least at least 260 Council votes (about 74%) out of a total of 352 by at least 15 Member States. Where the Council does not act on the basis of a Commission proposal, the QM threshold is the same, except that the votes in favour must be cast by at least two-thirds of the 28 Member States (i.e.19). In addition, a Member State may request verification that the QM represents at least 62% of the population of the EU.

A blocking minority must include at least four Member States, failing which the QM will be deemed attained. Any Member State can abstain at any time and abstentions count as no-votes (in unanimous voting, they do not prevent unanimity being reached, so they count as yes-votes).

The voting powers of the Member State governments in the Council are now based more on population than on the system of voting points negotiated with each EU enlargement. From 1 November 2014 a QM will be reached if a draft decision is supported by at least 55% of Member States (i.e. 16 member states), representing at least 65% of the EU population. Where the Council does not act on the basis of a Commission proposal, the QM threshold is 72% of Member States (i.e. 21), representing at least 65% of the EU population. Between 2014 and 2017 there will be a transitional phase where the new QMV rules apply, but where the old voting weights can be applied when a Member State requests it.

The increase in QMV has gone hand-in-hand with the extension of co-decision. The 1986 *Single European Act* (SEA) provisions on co-decision with QMV added a new dimension to the 'democratic deficit'".[157] The large increase in QMV allowed single market legislation to be adopted more easily

The European Union: A Democratic Institution? 105

in the Council, and so was regarded as efficient, but many opportunities for Member State governments to veto proposals were lost.[158] When the current transitional voting arrangements end, the post-2014 changes to weighted Council votes and what constitutes a QM will make mustering a blocking minority more difficult for non-Eurozone States. An *Open Europe* report in December 2011[159] noted that if the Eurozone votes as a caucus, non-euro States will never be able to form a blocking minority. Under the current voting rules, the Eurozone cannot form a QM on its own. After the voting rules change in 2014/17, if the Eurozone votes as a caucus, it will represent 66% of the EU population and will therefore achieve the threshold of 65% of the EU population needed to adopt a proposal. The Eurozone will have, as *Open Europe* put it, "a permanent in-built majority" in the Council, which "could leave the UK consistently outvoted on measures with a profound impact on its economy and the City of London, simply because it is outside this new inner core".

"Democracy requires political institutions that 'provide citizens with opportunities for political participation, influence and control'".

Robert Dahl, 'On Democracy', Connecticut: Yale University Press, 1999

---

4. PARTICIPATION BY EU CITIZENS AND CIVIL SOCIETY

4.1. EU Citizenship

A concept of EU citizenship has long been an EU aim. In 1985 the *Adonnino Committee* (chaired by Pietro Adonnino, Italian Christian Democrat MEP) proposed a "People's Europe" that would give citizens special rights and encourage them to develop a "European consciousness". Among its proposals were the notion of European citizenship, the European flag and anthem, the creation of a European Ombudsman and the right to vote and stand in local and EP elections. Many of these were later incorporated into the Maastricht Treaty, and have been enhanced by further reforms encouraging and providing for more citizen participation in EU affairs. EU citizenship was formally introduced in Article 2 of the Maastricht Treaty, which stated that the Union aims to "strengthen the protection of the rights and interests of the nationals of its Member States through the introduction of a citizenship of the Union". In addition to the established right to move, work and reside freely in any Member State, Maastricht introduced voting and election rights in EP and local elections, and extra consular protection for EU citizens. The *Treaty of Amsterdam* extended citizens' rights with a new anti-discrimination clause, while stipulating that Union citizenship "shall complement and not replace national citizenship".

The EU Treaty as amended by Lisbon states in Article 10(3)TEU that citizens have "the right to participate in the democratic life of the Union", and stipulates that "decisions shall be taken as openly and as closely as possible to the citizen". Yet, as noted in section 3(1) above, participatory democracy at EU level does not work well because the EU does not have decision-making structures into which citizens' contributions can be fed or acted upon.

EU citizenship is different from national citizenship. An EU Reflection Group report to the European Council on 5 December 1995 noted that although citizenship of the EU was "intended as a response to the need to involve citizens more closely in the process of European construction", there were differences of opinion on the concept in the Member States. In some, the concept of a complementary citizenship "was not readily understood"; while for supporters of a federal Europe, a common EU citizenship with clearly defined rights and obligations was essential.

The Lisbon Treaty asserted that EU citizenship does not replace national citizenship, but adds an extra layer of rights which are limited and defined by the EU Treaties and EU law. The terms of EU citizenship are set out in Articles 20-24 TFEU. Union citizenship does not generally entail any direct duties for citizens of the Union, "which constitutes a major difference between it and citizenship of the Member States".[160] Dr Annette Schrauwen maintains that: "In general, duties linked to Union citizenship are lacking": where national citizenship imposes duties, such as paying taxes or perhaps to vote, EU citizenship does not.[161] In a footnote Schrauwen clarifies: "The duty to obey European law is mostly indirect, via the national level. Citizens are only directly bound by European law in those instances where provisions have horizontal direct effect".[162] She concludes that "as long as there are no direct duties related to the status of Union citizenship, but only a bundle of rights, it will never have the same form as national citizenship and therefore will never completely replace national citizenship".[163]

Citizens of the EU cannot vote on matters of EU governance and the EU decision -making bodies do not respond directly to the concerns or views of citizens. However, the European Ombudsman investigates complaints from

The European Union: A Democratic Institution? 107

citizens about maladministration in the EU institutions, and the Commission's European Citizens' Initiative is an attempt to give citizens collectively an opportunity to influence EU policy-making. One of Damian Chalmers' suggestions was to empower EU citizens to "disapply" EU law via their national courts and parliaments:

> To protect certain domestic democratic values and traditions, citizens should have the right to petition a national Constitutional Court to disapply an EU law if the law violates those values or traditions. If an EU law is disapplied by a national parliament or Constitutional Council a majority of other parliaments, on the basis of an independent report, may petition the European Council to mediate, if the costs on other citizens are excessive or there is no violation of domestic democratic values or traditions.[164]

Some have suggested holding EU-wide referendums giving citizens the chance to overturn an existing EU law or to put a new legislative issue on the EU agenda. The Citizens' Initiative goes a small way towards this, but from a practical point of view, with an EU population of over 500 million and an electorate of around 375 million, the process would be highly complicated and would undoubtedly create unequal opportunities for 'disapplication'.

4.2. Civil Society

The *Treaty of Rome* provided a role for civil society in EU affairs through the European Economic and Social Committee (EESC). This EESC involves economic and social groups (but primarily economic groups) in establishing the common market, and it is the only way for interest groups (e.g. trade unionists, employers, farmers) to have a formal and institutionalised say on draft EU legislation. The EESC channels the views of interest groups to the larger EU institutions. The Commission's 2001 Governance White Paper thought the EESC could help tackle the democratic deficit and committed the EU to consulting and incorporating civil society in EU policy and decision-making. The Lisbon Treaty called on the EU institutions to have "open, transparent, and regular dialogue with representative associations and civil society" and the Commission is required to hold broad consultation with all concerned parties. The EESC's role has been enhanced by Treaty changes over the years, but it remains only a consultative body, and there have even been calls in recent years for the EESC and the other consultative body, the

Committee of the Regions, to be abolished.[165] In March 2011 the EESC held a seminar on the prospects for participatory democracy in Europe,[166] at the end of which the EESC concluded that it should work on the practical implementation of civil dialogue. The findings of the March 2013 *Flash Eurobarometer* report on Europeans' Engagement in Participatory Democracy suggest that around half those surveyed thought civil society could have some influence in the EU:

> Over half of the respondents in 19 Member States think that NGOs can influence EU decision-making -- At least 50% of people agree that NGOs can influence EU decision-making in 19 Member States, with a relatively high number of respondents saying this in Romania (71%), Portugal (68%) and Luxembourg and Denmark (both 66%).
>
> However, in six Member States a relative majority of people say that these organisations cannot influence EU-level decision-making: the Czech Republic (59% disagree vs. 37% who agree), Austria (54% vs. 42%), Slovenia (52% vs. 44%), Latvia (52% vs. 44%), Germany (48% vs. 46%) and the Netherlands (48% vs. 47%). Opinion is equally divided in Greece (49% agree and disagree).

4.3. Tackling the Euro Crisis

"... the crisis has transformed the EU from the "fantastic object" that inspired enthusiasm into something radically different. What was meant to be a voluntary association of equal states has now been transformed by the euro crisis into a relationship between creditor and debtor countries that is neither voluntary nor equal. Indeed, the euro could destroy the EU altogether".

George Soros, The W orld Economy's Shifting Challenges, Project Syndicate, 2 January 2014

The euro crisis has brought the subject of democratic legitimacy to the forefront of the debate on the future of Europe. It has had a major impact on the EU and its Member States, including non-Eurozone States, particularly with regard to the democratic legitimation by national parliaments of Commission, Council and European Central Bank measures to tackle the crisis. One expert commented that in the context of the ECB's Outright Monetary Transactions – OMT - programme), "In the EU, the rule of law, the

The European Union: A Democratic Institution? 109

separation of powers and democratic self-government have effectively been suspended", and he suggested that in the event of challenge, the Court of Justice would uphold any EU action that purported to end the euro crisis.[167]

In the 2012 Blueprint for a deep and genuine economic and monetary union, the Commission insisted on a "a robust democratic framework" for the deepening of Economic and Monetary Union (EMU) and on ensuring "optimal democratic accountability and governance". It set out two basic principles for the EU's democratic legitimacy in moves to deepen EMU in order to help solve the euro crisis:

> First, in multilevel governance systems, accountability should be ensured at that level where the respective executive decision is taken, whilst taking due account of the level where the decision has an impact. Second, in developing EMU as in European integration generally, the level of democratic legitimacy always needs to remain commensurate with the degree of transfer of sovereignty from Member States to the European level.
>
> This holds true for new powers on budgetary surveillance and economic policy as much as for new EU rules on solidarity between Member States. Briefly put: Further financial mutualisation requires commensurate political integration.

But the crisis seems to have reinforced the two-tier economic integration structure of Eurozone and non-Eurozone States, with many of the new rules and structures that deal with the euro crisis becoming Eurozone-specific. Many observers believe the role and weight of the new Eurogroup will increase rather than decrease. Margarida Vasconcelos[168] http://www. europeanfoundation.org/my_weblog/2013/03/margarida-vasconcelos-brussels-must-start-listening-to-people-democratic-wishes.htmlthought the EU's response to the financial crisis through austerity measures, and its moves to control Eurozone States' economic and fiscal policies, had led to a further democratic deficit and lack of legitimacy at both European and national levels. The sovereignty of Eurozone States, she thought, would be further reduced with full fiscal and political union, "with an economic policy imposed by Germany", and no possibility of rejecting it.[169] In an article in the *Financial Times* Tony Barber thought some Eurozone members were facing a new and difficult reality:

> In debtor countries such as Greece and Spain, but also in states such as France and Italy that drag their heels on reform, the perception is taking hold that society is at the mercy of pitiless external forces – Germany or

globalisation, bankers or Brussels – and is being punished for the misguided prescriptions of outsiders.[170]

The Eurocrisis has raised questions about whether the EU, representing 28 Member States, can legitimately make fiscal and banking decisions for the 17-Member Eurozone, "given that the issues at stake go to the heart of national sovereignty on taxation, spending and borrowing"?[171] The measures the EU has taken to mitigate the crisis have given rise to criticism that traditional budgetary sovereignty has been undermined, that elected politicians in the States worst affected have been sidelined by Commission, ECB and IMF technocrats, and that Germany not only called all the shots but profited from the crisis.[172]

Even László Andor, the Commissioner for Employment, Social Affairs and Inclusion, thought the situation might become so bad for some southern European states that "Eurozone membership and democracy are no longer compatible".[173]

Ben Crum told the Lords inquiry into the Role of National Parliaments in the EU that during the crisis, "the operating conditions of debtor state parliaments have been severely constrained, to the point of compromising the very idea of representative democracy". He called for Treaty provisions "that guarantee the continued respect for, and effective functioning of, national parliaments in countries that are bailed out and find "Memorandums of Understanding" imposed upon them".[174]

The Lords EU Committee report, Genuine Economic and Monetary Union' and the implications for the UK,[175] concluded (para. 143) that "There is a risk that top-down control removes the power from citizens to determine at the ballot box how taxes are raised and public money is spent in their country. Ensuring democratic legitimacy for the evolving system of economic governance is crucial", but the Committee left detailed discussion of this to the Lords report on the role of national parliaments in the EU.

5. DEALING WITH THE DEMOCRATIC DEFICIT

5.1. Introduction

Few dispute the existence of a democratic deficit in the EU's institutional and decision - making systems, although there is disagreement over the degree of the deficit. Simon Hix described the EU as a "semi or non-democratic institution";[176] Bill Cash believes there exists not a democratic deficit but a "democratic crisis"[177] Andrew Moravcsik, on the other hand, thinks the EU is as democratic as it can be. There is also a vast array of opinion both from eurosceptics and EU supporters on how to tackle the deficit, ranging from abolishing the EU altogether, turning it into a 'United States of Europe' with a f ully federal system, giving national governments and/or parliaments more powers. Some of these suggestions are considered below.

The EU charts Treaty amendments that have already sought to tackle the democratic deficit, by reinforcing the EP's powers, improving transparency and encouraging citizen participation in EU projects and consultations. The Lisbon Treaty opened up Council sessions to the public, strengthened the powers of the EP in legislative and budgetary matters, involved it in the appointment of the Commission President, improved citizen participation through the citizens' initiative and Treaty recognition of the importance of dialogue between the EU institutions and civil society.

Andrew Moravcsik[178] maintained in 2006 – before the Lisbon reforms - that further channels of democratic legitimisation were not required; the EU, he said, was the product of an intergovernmental agreement embodied in the EU Treaties that is "pragmatically efficient, normatively attractive and politically stable".[179] Moravcsik thought the EU was a satisfactory negotiated equilibrium, periodically modified when the need arose, and otherwise reconfirmed, and that it therefore reflected the requirements of participating states. He also believed that increasing the opportunities to participate and decide would not necessarily generate more participation and that increased participation would not necessarily generate more legitimisation. In his view, declining voter participation in EP elections appeared to confirm that the greater scope for democratic participation provided for by the Treaties had largely been unused; and that where and when it had been used, this had been to express dissatisfaction with the domestic policies of national governments.[180] Moravcsik attributed this situation to the nature of the tasks undertaken by the EU, such as international trade, development assistance, agriculture and safety standards for goods and services, which had modest general political salience for most citizens.

Stefano Micossi[181] has argued that the EU is generally no better or worse than its component states when it comes to being democratic, "even if multiple, and potentially conflicting legitimisation channels and principles may confuse observers".[182] Micossi refutes the argument that the EU cannot have democratic legitimacy because it has no *demos*, no common identity or "sufficiently shared values to guide institutional and political action":

True, a weak common identity makes it difficult to refer back to a single popular support base; but it does not preclude the development of partial mechanisms legitimising individual decisions or decision-making processes, through national parliaments, the European Parliament, and various other channels participating in the process. Nor does it preclude forms of legitimisation linked to the output of common action, insofar as the said action does meet voters' needs that individual national states are no longer in a position to satisfy.

Hix and Follesdal believe the increased politicisation of the Council and EP signals a change that could give the EU more democratic legitimacy:

> Democratic contestation, in terms of trans-national alignments and coalitions along left–right lines have started to emerge in both the EU Council and the European Parliament. What is still missing, though, is the connection between these developments and the divisions in the EU's society at large, in terms of the potential winners and losers of potential policy agendas. This may not even require fundamental reform of the EU treaties. All that may be needed is for the political elites to make a commitment to open the door to more politicization of the EU agenda, for example via a battle for the Commission President, with governments and national and European parties backing different candidates and policy platforms. European Parliament elections would continue to be primarily 'second-order' for some time. But, if there are new incentives for national party leaders to compete in these contests on European-level issues rather than purely national concerns, over time EU-wide coalitions and alignments between national and European actors would begin to solidify.[183]

However, other analysts think concrete reforms are in order, some requiring Treaty change, others not. Charles Grant, of the *Centre for European Reform*, suggests the EU could improve its "outputs" to restore its legitimacy in the eyes of citizens, but also that EU governance is "in bad need of an overhaul".[184] He thinks national legislatures need to be more involved in Eurozone governance, but also that they will have to "think European" in the way that heads of government have learnt to do in the European Council. His suggestions f or improving democratic legitimacy include strengthening the 'yellow card' system to allow national parliaments to force the Commission to withdraw a proposal and establishing a forum for national parliamentarians in Brussels.

In September 2012 the final report of the *Future of Europe Group* (the Foreign Ministers of Austria, Belgium, Denmark, France, Italy, Germany,

The European Union: A Democratic Institution? 113

Luxembourg, the Netherlands, Poland, Portugal and Spain) included a proposal for "a directly elected Commission President who personally appoints the members of his 'European Government', a European Parliament with the powers to initiate legislation and a second chamber for the Member States".[185] In evidence to the Lords EU Committee inquiry, Professor Stelio Mangiameli, University of Teramo, thought national parliaments should have an EU-based role: "if there is a political will ... it is not exaggerated to state that there is scope for giving rise to a general overhaul of the European constitutional architecture, that may lead to an actual representation of national parliaments within the form of government of the European Union ...".

Damian Chalmers (LSE) proposes democracy tests which he thinks would not require Treaty change:

1. There should be a new test of relative democratic authority where the EU can only act if it enlarges choices or protects certain values in a way that cannot be done by domestic parliaments and where the benefits of this action exceed collective domestic democratic costs.
2. This test of relative democratic authority would be policed by national parliaments. An EU proposal would be abandoned unless two thirds of the national parliaments indicate their support.
3. A new test of democratic responsiveness would require that if one third of the national parliaments propose either that legislation be reviewed or that new legislation should be proposed, the Commission is obliged to make a proposal to this effect.
4. Individual national parliaments should also be able to pass laws disapplying EU law where an independent study shows that EU law imposes higher costs than benefits for that member state.[186]

Some of these suggestions, and others, are discussed in more detail in the following sections.

5.2. More 'Differentiation' in the EU?

Would a more democratic EU be one in which there were more options for individual Member States to go their own way in areas of particular importance to them – i.e. more differentiation? There is already a mix of alternative arrangements, some temporary, some indefinite, that have been agreed during accession or Treaty amendment negotiations:

- Temporary transitional provisions governing the accession of new Member State s (covering varying elements of the *acquis communautaire*);
- Opt-outs established in Treaty revisions and protocols to EU Treaties (likely to be long-term or permanent, e.g. UK from EMU, Schengen and elements of Justice and Home Affairs (JHA) + earlier from social policy; Denmark from EMU, Common Security and Defence Policy (CSDP) and JHA); [187]
- EMU obligation: new Member States must adopt the euro providing they meet the Maastricht Treaty criteria;[188]
- Other protocol-based arrangements on Treaty application: UK, Poland, Czech Republic and Charter of Fundamental Rights (not strictly speaking an opt-out);
- Opt-in protocol: UK and Ireland re. JHA; Enhanced cooperation (with at least nine Member States and only within shared competences, e.g. trans-European divorce law, EU patent; financial transaction tax);
- Permanent structured cooperation (PESCO - only within CSDP: authorised by Council by QMV at request of participating States; no Member State threshold for establishing PESCO);
- Cooperation on the basis of international law: e.g. Schengen, Prüm Convention, the Treaty on Stability, Coordination and Governance in the Economic and Monetary Union (fiscal compact treaty);
- Open Method of Coordination: the voluntary cooperation of Member States, based on soft law mechanisms such as guidelines, indicators, benchmarking and sharing of best practice (e.g. Euro Plus Pact of March 2011).

The table below shows how EU Member State currently participate in differentiated integration, i.e. where certain EU rules do not apply in some Member States?[189]

Perhaps the way forward for a more democratic EU is more flexibility; an EU of 'concentric circles', with groups of Member States doing more of what they want to do and less of what they don't want to do in many variations of enhanced cooperation. But this too may present risks and a potential threat to legitimacy, as David Lidington acknowledged before the December 2011 European Council.[190] There was, he thought, a small risk that an intergovernmental solution to the Eurozone crisis involving the 17 Eurozone States and some others could have the effect of "caucusing on single market measures", presenting the UK with a "take it or leave it" option.[191]

At the end of May 2013, a joint Franco-German letter,[192] floated ideas such as a eurozone budget, a bank resolution regime, contracts for economic reform and a permanent president for the Eurogroup. The two governments proposed "contractual arrangements", agreements in which Member States would commit to structural reform in exchange for financial support from a new "fiscal capacity" (i.e. a Eurozone budget): "Member States and the European level will enter into contractual arrangements. Both sides will be committed to implement the undertakings under these contractual arrangements". This could be the basis for future Eurozone economic governance, but it could also affect the functioning of the whole EU.

The Commission published a Communication in March 2013[193] outlining its idea of contractual arrangements "combined with a solidarity mechanism for national structural reforms for competitiveness and growth whose lack of implementation would have a spillover effect on other Member States but whose implementation would need to be done by the Member State concerned under particular stress".

The Commission would have the central role (which the Franco-German paper had not given it): negotiating the details of the plan, monitoring implementation of the arrangement annually as part the European Semester, and assessing progress. The Commission would give national parliaments and social partners a role in the process:

> In all circumstances, national parliaments should be involved before the endorsement of the contractual arrangements by the Council. Where appropriate, and depending on the specific nature of the envisaged reforms, other national stakeholders such as social partners should also be involved. Where relevant and appropriate, representatives of the Commission would be available to participate in dialogue with national parliaments on the application of the instrument.

But this kind of intergovernmentalism and differentiation raises other questions about democratic legitimacy, as Piotr Buras[194] points out in The EU's Silent Revolution:

> For example, if member states are required to commit through contractual arrangements to undertake structural reforms in exchange for financial support, who decides on the reforms? The imposition of reforms by Brussels would strengthen "technocratic federalism". If, on the other hand, they were designed by national governments but a new government would be bound by them, it would limit the space for political discretion and thus

violate democratic rules even more than in the current system. The deeper integration of the eurozone also raises questions about how to secure democratic accountability and public scrutiny of policies there by using institutions designed for the whole EU. Should the whole European Parliament perform tasks also in the areas which do not affect all EU member states? Building new parliamentary structures for the eurozone may be the only solution – with far-reaching consequences for the whole institutional structure of the EU.[195]

Overview

Participation of EU Member States in projects of differentiated integration

Projects	AT	BE	BG	CY	CZ	DE	DK	EE	ES	FI	FR	GB	GR	HU	IE	IT	LT	LU	LV	MT	NL	PL	PT	RO	SE	SI	SK	Total
Eurozone	1	1	0	1	0	1	0	1	1	1	1	0	1	0	1	1	0	1	0	1	1	0	1	0	0	1	1	17
Euro Plus Pact	1	1	1	1	0	1	1	1	1	1	1	0	1	0	1	1	1	1	1	1	1	1	1	1	0	1	1	23
Fiscal Pact	1	1	1	1	0	1	1	1	1	1	1	0	1	1	1	1	1	1	1	1	1	1	1	1	1	1	1	25
CSDP	1	1	1	1	1	1	0	1	1	1	1	1	1	1	1	1	1	1	1	1	1	1	1	1	1	1	1	26
Schengen Agreement[a]	1	1	1	1	1	1	1	1	1	1	1	0	1	1	0	1	1	1	1	1	1	1	1	1	1	1	1	25
Charta of Fundamental Rights	1	1	1	1	0	1	1	1	1	1	1	0	1	1	1	1	1	1	1	1	1	0	1	1	1	1	1	24
AFSJ[b]	1	1	1	1	1	1	0	1	1	1	1	0	1	1	0	1	1	1	1	1	1	1	1	1	1	1	1	24
EU Patent	1	1	1	1	1	1	1	1	1	0	1	1	1	1	1	1	0	1	1	1	1	1	1	1	1	1	1	25
Trans European Divorce Law	1	1	1	0	0	1	0	0	1	0	1	0	0	1	0	1	0	1	1	1	0	0	1	1	0	1	0	14
Total	9	9	8	8	4	9	6	8	8	8	9	2	8	7	6	9	8	9	9	9	8	6	9	8	6	9	8	

a Bulgaria, Romania, and Cyprus ratified the Schengen Agreement, but it has not entered fully into force.

b Opt-outs with an opt-in possibility are treated in this table as non-participation.

Source: author's compilation.

The Lords EU Committee wanted national parliaments to have "more effective purchase on the steps towards enhanced economic surveillance":

> Means must be found to ensure that EU institutions are accountable not only to the European Parliament but also to national parliaments, in particular when such significant decisions about their future are being taken. Further steps towards greater eurozone integration are likely to follow in the years to come. Unless steps are taken to strengthen national parliaments' role in oversight of such developments, the democratic foundations of the EU could be undermined.[196]

This situation also presents the EU with a 'West Lothian question'. Dr Joanne Hunt of Cardiff University pointed out in evidence to the Lords EU Committee inquiry:

The European Union: A Democratic Institution? 117

If MEPs elected by States outside the eurozone (or other area of flexible/differentiated integration) are not to be permitted to participate in democratic control of activities, what additional or better claims do national parliaments from non participating states have to be included? Should national parliaments be excluded from exercising the right to participate and 'vote' through the EWS on measures that are not going to apply to their state? How should the EU answer this particular version of the West Lothian question?

Open Europe is also sceptical, commenting that the Eurozone crisis "is forcing its 17 members closer together, with a risk that these countries start to act and vote as a 'caucus' in areas which do not directly relate to eurozone governance".[197]

The German finance minister, Wolfgang Schäuble, wrote in a joint article with George Osborne in the *Financial Times* on 27 March 2014 that any EU Treaty change must "guarantee fairness" for countries outside the eurozone. While Mats Persson, director of Open Europe, thought this marked "a substantial win for Osborne and Cameron", how reliable would German support for a democratic form of differentiation turn out to be?

5.3. A Bigger Role for National Parliaments?

> "There is widespread agreement that national parliaments – individually the cornerstone of any constitutional democracy - may be able to provide an effective and convincing way of shoring up the democratic legitimacy gaps which are perceived to exist within the EU order.
>
> With the EU's political and legal framework having privileged the position of central governments, national parliaments may be considered to have been sidelined and marginalized, and their democratic legitimating function not adequately fulfilled by the European Parliament. Despite imaginative scholarly attempts to present the Union as demanding and deserving models of legitimation which break with traditional ideas of representative democracy, the latter's appeal has continued to survive".
>
> Dr Joanne Hunt, W ritten evidence, 2 October 2013

Is the solution to the democratic deficit to be found in giving national MPs, rather than MEPs, more power? This is the UK Government's view, which is considered in more detail in Section 6 below.

The Lisbon Treaty gave new powers to national parliaments in an Early Warning Mechanism (EWM) to alert the Commission to possible subsidiarity breaches, but some analysts are critical of the actual effect of this.

In evidence to the Lords Inquiry into the Role of National Parliaments in the EU, the Finnish *Eduskunta* thought nothing much had changed with Lisbon:

> While it is good that more national parliaments have taken an active role in EU affairs since the Lisbon treaty, we see no evidence that the inputs of national parliaments have actually affected outcomes at the EU level. We fear that the post-Lisbon arrangements have created the appearance but not the reality of increased parliamentary participation.

But its view was that Member States needed to provide democratic legitimacy by tackling relations between governments and parliaments. This did not require Treaty change; it was a matter for national parliaments to resolve: "democratic legitimacy in the EU requires that each national parliament controls its country's EU policy to the full extent of that parliament's powers under the national constitution. This can only be achieved within each member state".

Not all EU national parliaments are equally engaged with the EU. They scrutinise their governments in different ways (see also below) and, as Professor Adam Cygan told the Lords Inquiry on the Role of National Parliaments in the EU they do not exist "as a collective bloc which acts as some form of 'revising chamber within the EU legislative process... and the Article 12 TEU requirement of 'actively contributing to the good functioning of the Union' is undoubtedly interpreted differently within the national parliaments.[198] It is difficult to see how allowing national parliaments more powers to block 'unwanted' legislation work in practice.

What is unwanted for one parliament is not necessarily so for another; EU agreement is almost always based on a compromise.

The EU has gradually reduced national vetoes in the Council in order to prevent endless wrangling among Member States and to facilitate the adoption of legislation. Giving national parliaments such powers could lead to legislative gridlock. Professor Hix is not averse to gridlock, as he told the Lords EU Committee: "Gridlock is not a bad thing if it means broader

The European Union: A Democratic Institution? 119

consensus and deliberation. I think history has shown the longer it takes to make decisions often they can be better decisions".[199]

On 17 October 2013 the Netherlands *Tweede Kamer* (Lower House) published a report on the *Democratic Legitimacy in the EU and the role of national parliaments*, with proposals to enhance the yellow card procedure, and introducing 'green card' and 'late card' mechanisms. The report proposed three ways to boost the yellow card:

- Extend the period during which parliaments can object beyond the current eight weeks;
- Broaden the grounds on which parliaments can object to EU laws to propo rtionality and the legal base of the proposal;
- Lower the threshold for the number of parliaments required to activate the yellow card

Open Europe summarised the Dutch mechanisms as follows:

'Green card': This new mechanism would allow national parliaments to *propose* new policies to the European Commission, including the amendment or repeal of existing EU laws. This would make national parliaments 'agenda-setters' in the EU decision-making process, as opposed to the current situation in which they can only react to proposals originating in Brussels. At present, only the Commission can make proposals to scrap EU laws.

'Late card': This would give national parliaments the right to object to proposals *at the end* of negotiations between the European Commission, the Council of Ministers and MEPs. At the moment, national parliaments can only examine a proposal when the Commission has tabled it. However, the final product can often look completely different. For example, the bankers' bonus cap was introduced by MEPs and wasn't in the version of the proposal on capital requirements national parliaments received from the European Commission.[200]

The report also considered ways of getting national MPs to work more closely together "and so act as a counterweight to the Commission's and the European Parliament's centralising tendencies".

The Lords EU Committee broadly supported the 'green card' idea, with a proviso: it "would need to include an undertaking by the Commission that it would consider such suggestions carefully, and either bring forward appropriate legislative or other proposals (or consult on them), or explain why it had decided not to take the requested action".[201]

Not all analysts believe that national parliaments have a legitimate role in EU decision - making. In evidence to the Lords EU Committee, Oskar Josef Gstrein and Darren Harvey[202] maintained EU law was for EU institutions to make, but that the levels of decision-making should be clarified:

> ... it has to be clearly acknowledged that legislative procedures on the EU level will never be "as close" to the European citizen as their national equivalents. More importantly, however, it is questionable if understanding the issue of "democratic legitimacy" in this way is appropriate, since it is not the purpose of European institutions to replace those already existing at the national level. Clearly, it is the task of European legislation to solve European problems. Nothing more and nothing less. Therefore, it is wrong to include national parliaments in the process of European legislation as such. However, what is necessary is an improved procedure in order to clarify the sphere for national and European legislation. It is time to transform the principle of subsidiarity from a political token gesture into a legally feasible concept.

5.4. Better Parliamentary Scrutiny of the EU

Scrutiny of the EU by national parliaments is potentially a useful and influential tool, but its effectiveness depends both on the powers of national parliaments in relation to their governments and in relation to the EU decision-making processes. Do national parliaments scrutinise or exert control over the EU or their governments sufficiently or effectively? Is better scrutiny the key to transparency and legitimacy in the EU? Should all national parliaments seek to adopt the strong mandating model of EU scrutiny of the Danish *Folketing* (national parliaments in the new Member States have all copied this model)?

In 1995 the Reflection Group Report on Treaty change recommended more transparency in decision-making processes, so that national parliaments could more effectively scrutinise what the EU was doing. This led in 1997 to the *Protocol on the role of national parliaments* in the Amsterdam Treaty, which has been strengthened in subsequent Treaty changes. The Lisbon Treaty provided for 'yellow card' and 'orange card' warning processes when national parliaments object to a proposal on subsidiarity grounds. Lisbon also called on national parliaments to "contribute actively to the good functioning of the Union" by:

- being informed by the EU institutions and having draft EU legislative acts forwarded to them;

The European Union: A Democratic Institution? 121

- making sure the principle of subsidiarity is respected;
- taking part, within the framework of the area of freedom, security and justice, in the evaluation mechanisms for the implementation of EU policies in this area;
- being involved in the political monitoring of Europol and the evaluation of Eurojust's activities;
- taking part in the revision procedures of the Treaties;
- being notified of applications for accession to the Union;
- monitoring EU proposals on family law, with the power for any national parliament to veto them;
- taking part in inter-parliamentary cooperation between national parliaments and with the EP.[203]

The Protocol also provides that a national parliament may bring a case before the EU Court of Justice, arguing that an adopted legislative act does not comply with the principle of subsidiarity. This has been called a 'red card' procedure, but it is different from the 'red card' national veto the Government has proposed (see Section 6.3 below).

Follesdal and Hix concede that EU integration "has meant an increase in executive power and a decrease in national parliamentary control", but maintain that the deficit is the result of governments acting in the Council without recourse to their national parliaments or parliamentary scrutiny:

> At the domestic level in Europe, the central structure of representative government in all EU Member States is that the government is accountable to the voters via the parliament. European parliaments may have few formal powers of legislative amendment (unlike the US Congress). But, the executive is held to account by the parliament that can hire and fire the cabinet, and by parliament scrutiny of the behaviour of government ministers. The design of the EU means that policy-making at the European is dominated by executive actors: national ministers in the Council, and government appointees in the Commission. This, by itself, is not a problem.
>
> However, the actions of these executive agents at the European level are beyond the control of national parliaments. Even with the establishment of European Affairs Committees in all national parliaments, ministers when speaking and voting in the Council, national bureaucrats when making policies in Coreper or Council working groups, and officials in the Commission when drafting or implementing legislation, are much more isolated from national parliamentary scrutiny and control than are national cabinet ministers or bureaucrats in the domestic policy-making process. As a

result, governments can effectively ignore their parliaments when making decisions in Brussels. Hence, European integration has meant a decrease in the power of national parliaments and an increase in the power of executives.[204]

Their view is that the democratic deficit lies as much with national governance as with EU governance, and it is the responsibility of national parliaments to scrutinise their governments better. But national parliaments have different ideas about their role in the democratic process. In evidence to the Lords EU Committee inquiry, Claudia Hefftler, Valentin Kreilinger, Olivier Rozenberg and Wolfgang Wessels identified seven models of parliamentary control: the "limited control model", the "Europe as usual" model, the "expert model", the "public forum", the "government accountability" model, the "policy maker", and "full Europeanisation". The differences between Member States are rooted in their visions of what the role of a parliament in a democracy should be. The authors emphasised that it was essential "to combine room for manoeuvre of the head of state or government with deeply informed oversight by national parliaments", and this was for national governments and parliaments to work out between them.

But good national scrutiny will not by itself resolve the democratic deficit, as Simon Hix acknowledged in evidence to the ESC on 12 June 2013. Referring to the "weaknesses of the aspiration" that strengthening the scrutiny powers of national parliaments over their national governments is a way to close the democratic deficit, he emphasised how difficult it was to get early information about what is going on in the EU institutions. He thought the Council was still too secretive and operated "primarily very much as a diplomatic body, rather than seeing itself as a legislative body".[205]

Richard Yung, a member of the European Affairs Committee in the French Senate, told the Lords EU Committee[206] that there should be more exchanges of information between national parliaments and the Commission, especially before budgetary decisions are made, a greater flow of information between national parliaments and the Commission, and more exchanges between national parliaments. But should national parliaments necessarily have a role in the EU legislative process? Heleen Jalvingh, UCL School for Public Policy, did not think so. She told the Lords EU Committee that most national parliament tasks "are focused on scrutinising legislation rather than having a legislative role. For that reason, therefore, their task at EU level should be limited to scrutinising EU policies rather than shaping actual EU decisions".[207]

She believed the Lisbon provisions suffice, given the limited resources of national parliaments, and that the EP was better equipped than national parliaments to deal with EU dossiers. She concluded: "Rather than increasing NPs' powers in EU decision-making, which would eventually paralyze EU decision-making, the most important and necessary change to the Treaty is to increase transparency within the Council".

Should national parliaments coordinate their scrutiny of governments before important intergovernmental summits in order to jointly hold the executive to account before intergovernmental decisions are taken? Could there be a joint scrutiny committee of national parliaments from all EU Member States, where views could be garnered more quickly during the eight weeks parliaments have to scrutinise proposals and submit yellow cards under the early warning mechanism? Lord Harrison asked how national parliaments could "combine in an effective way, in terms of resources and time [...] and in terms of consulting 28 member states, as well as those states consulting the Commission or, in some cases, the European Central Bank" in order to remedy the democratic deficit.[208]

In evidence to the Lords EU Committee on 22 October 2013, Professor Adam Cygan thought national EU scrutiny committees were not thorough enough, that they needed to "start going further upstream, looking at impact assessment and going directly to the Commission at source to consider what the Commission is using as justification for legislation ". He also pointed to the challenge of scrutinising EU 'soft law': policy co-ordination and the use of complementary competencies. He cited Europe 2020 as an example, noting that "These have regulatory, financial, political impacts across the member states and they are not open to systematic review.

Professor Hix thought the Committee's role "should be one of scrutinising the whole legislative process from the Commission's initiation through what happens inside the Parliament through to the Council".[209]

Something else to bear in mind is that not all national parliaments have the same scrutiny powers, and in some Member States strengthening national parliaments means strengthening governments, which is not the same.

In its report on Reforming the European Scrutiny System in the House of Commons in November 2013, the European Scrutiny Committee recommended among other things for the requirement for a European Reporter to be appointed on each Departmental Select Committee to be written into Standing Orders, and a more systematic approach to scrutinising the Commission Work Programme:

209. We recommend that the House, through the European Scrutiny Committee and Departmental Select Committees, produces a document along the lines of the Netherlands model. All Departmental Select Committees would be expected to set out which of the proposals in the Programme they will aim to scrutinise, forming the basis for a debate which takes place in the House at the beginning of the Work Programme period. Should a Departmental Select Committee indicate to us that it saw a document as particularly worthy of debate, we would take account of that. We as a Committee would also continue to review the Work Programme. The Government would then use this information as a basis for making commitments to hold debates on particular documents, following discussions with this Committee (and without prejudice to our right to refer documents for debate). The Work Programme for the coming year is usually published in the autumn and comes into effect in January, so the timeframe for doing this would typically be November and December. We would publish a Report for debate on the floor of the House setting out our priorities and those of the Departmental Select Committees.

In evidence to the Lords EU Committee, the Europe Minister said the Government wanted to focus on "the most important issues" and apply "lighter touch" scrutiny for less significant EU documents. He also reiterated calls for further mainstreaming of EU business and greater engagement of departmental select committees, as in Germany.[210]

5.5. More Interparliamentary Cooperation?

The Lisbon Treaty provided for a strengthening of interparliamentary cooperation mechanisms, connected in particular with the Conference of Speakers of EU Parliaments, which meets once a year and which produces guidelines for interparliamentary cooperation (IPC). Is IPC the best way for the EP and national parliaments to help legitimise EU policy - making, through participation in discussion and debate, at, for example, the Conference of Speakers of the EU parliaments and COSAC, or through sectoral joint committees, exchange of best practice, the EU Interparliamentary Exchange (IPEX), and the European Centre for Parliamentary Research and Documentation (ECPRD)? The aim of IPC is:

a) To promote the exchange of information and best practices between the national parliaments of the European Parliament with a view to reinforcing parliamentary control, influence and scrutiny at all levels.

b) To ensure effective exercise of parliamentary competences in EU matters in particular in the area of monitoring the principles of subsidiarity and proportionality.

c) To promote cooperation with parliaments from third countries.[211]

IPC cannot make or amend EU legislation, but delegates can exert pressure on the Commission to initiate legislation or reform. The Guidelines for Inter-parliamentary Cooperation in the European Union of June 2008 sets out a framework for IPC, and some of its components are considered below.

A Stronger COSAC?

In 1989 the *Conférence des Organes Spécialisés dans les Affaires Communautaires*, or COSAC, was established. The Speakers of the Member State parliaments agreed to strengthen the role of national parliaments in relation to Community matters by bringing together their Committees on European Affairs. COSAC was formally recognised in the Amsterdam Treaty *Protocol on the Role of National Parliaments in the European Union* which came into force 1 May 1999. The Lisbon Treaty gave it more powers: under Article 10 of the Protocol on the Role of National Parliaments, COSAC:

> ... may submit any contribution it deems appropriate for the attention of the European Parliament, the Council and the Commission. The Conference shall in addition promote the exchange of information and best practice between national Parliaments and the European Parliament, including their special committees. It may also organise interparliamentary conferences on specific topics, in particular to debate matters of common foreign and security policy, including common security and defence policy. Contributions from the Conference shall not bind national Parliaments and shall not prejudge their positions.

COSAC and EP representatives meet twice a year, usually in the capital of the country holding the rotating EU Presidency. The Commission has acknowledged the important role of COSAC in the political dialogue between it and national parliaments. COSAC is a platform for national parliaments to share views and exchange information, but its role is limited, its contributions non-binding, and, as Steve Pryce has noted, it "scarcely contributes to closing the EU's "parliamentary deficit", and there has been little appetite to give it "a more robust mandate".[212] In evidence to the Lords EU Committee inquiry, the Finnish *Eduskunta* was doubtful about 'dialogue' delivering results for national parliaments, but called for better provision of information between the Commission and national parliaments:

> The concept of "dialogue" among institutions needs to be examined more closely. It seems doubtful whether there can really exist a "dialogue" in the sense of an on-going exchange of views between a large bureaucracy like the Commission and the 39 chambers, each comprising scores or hundreds of vocal and opinionated individuals, that we call parliaments. Any "dialogue" would probably involve either a formalised exchange of generally phrased letters or be controlled by a small group of individuals acting in the name of their respective institution. The first is ineffective, the latter risks being opaque and undemocratic.
>
> We believe that it would be helpful to replace the concept of "dialogue" with that of information flows, inputs and outcomes: Parliaments need better access to the Commission's reasoning. The Commission should inform itself of reactions to its proposals. Parliaments' inputs need to be channelled to the places where the decisions are taken.

COSAC and several Member State parliaments including the UK's would like a gre ater role for national parliaments in the EU decision-making process in order to legitimise it. At the COSAC meeting in Vilnius on 27–29 October 2013, the UK delegation tabled an amendment calling for "a full debate on the strengthening of democratic legitimacy of the Union and the fundamental role of national Parliaments for the good functioning of the Union as well as on how this role could be further enhanced". The Vilnius Conclusions expressed the need to fundamentally re-examine democratic legitimacy in Europe, and hoped for a "full debate on the strengthening of democratic legitimacy of the Union and the fundamen tal role of national Parliaments for the good functioning of the Union as well as on how this role could be further enhanced".

Interparliamentary Conferences?

The Parliament of the Member State that holds the six-monthly EU Presidency can organise conferences with the chairs of specialised EP committees, such as the committees on budget and finance, agriculture etc and delegations from national parliaments. At the Conference of Speakers of EU Parliaments in April 2012, an Inter-Parliamentary Conference for the Common Foreign and Security Policy (CFSP) and the Common Security and Defence Policy (CSDP) was established. It provides a framework for the exchange of information and best practice in the areas of CFSP and CSDP, to enable national Parliaments and the European Parliament to be fully informed in this policy area. Delegates may by consensus adopt non-binding conclusions.

The Interparliamentary Conference is composed of delegations from national parliaments and the EP (national parliaments are represented by six Members each; the EP by sixteen Members. EU candidate countries and European NATO members can be represented by a delegation of 4 observers). However, the membership question has already given rise to disputes between the EP and national parliaments over which has the most competence and which should have a larger representation. The *Inter-parliamentary Conference on Economic and Financial Governance* (EFG) met in October 2013 in Vilnius. The Conference conclusions confirmed that:

> ... democratic control and accountability should take place at the level where decisions are taken and implemented; this implies a pivotal role for national Parliaments in controlling the implementation of the relevant policies at the national level, in ensuring the legitimacy of Member State actions in the European Council and the Council, and in the conduct of national fiscal, economic and social policies, while the European Parliament is a co-legislator and ensures scrutiny and democratic accountability for the decisions taken at the Union level;[213]

The Conference launched the "Vilnius Process", by which a working group open to national parliaments and the EP would by consensus draw up practical arrangements and rules of procedure. The conference would not be an extension of COSAC; it would focus on information exchange and coordination, not adopting conclusions and common positions. However, as the Austrian MEP, Othmar Karas, observed in the case of the EFG interparliamentary conference, it seemed that the more competence the EP had, the more "annoying" national parliaments found the EP. At the second EFG inter-parliamentary conference in January 2014, Bill Cash emphasised the relative roles of national parliaments and the EP in providing democratic legitimacy, and called for the balance of power to be returned to the national parliaments. The EP President, Martin Schulz, agreed that reform would be necessary, but in his view the purpose would be to ensure a true transnational democracy; the role of the EP could not and should not be called into question.

Competing Parliaments?

How willing are the EP and national parliaments to cooperate in what should be the common objective of scrutinising the Commission? Simon Hix told the Lords EU Committee he did not accept the idea that there is the EP "on the one side and national parliaments on the other side, and there is some sort of battle between the two about who gets to scrutinise what. Both are parliamentary institutions".

Dr Julie Smith described how national parliaments and the EP were all busy writing reports on EU policies, talking to the same people, "re -inventing the wheel very often", but none of them were exchanging information or collaborating.

RELATIONS BETWEEN THE EP AND NATIONAL PARLIAMENTS

Two recent events show how far the EP and national parliaments are from agreeing an arrangement that could contribute to improving the EU's democratic credentials. On 11 February 2014 the EP Constitutional Affairs Committee (AFCO) discussed a draft report by the Italian EPP MEP, Carlo Casini, on relations between the EP and national parliaments. The report focused on national parliament cooperation in, rather than control of, EU decision-making. The primary task of national parliaments was, it emphasised, to monitor, control and provide democratic legitimacy to the Council. The report put the onus on national parliaments to improve their scrutiny of national governments and to provide the latter with prior guidance on their work in the Council.

The report recommended a legal framework and more formal procedures for the emerging EU inter-parliamentary system and suggested upgrading the role of the annual Conference of Speakers. In the ensuing debate, there was clear disagreement among MEPs over what UK Liberal Democrat MEP Andrew Duff thought was the blurring of the separation of powers between the EU and national levels.

Some MEPs pointed to the rivalry between the EP and national parliaments, and the unlikelihood of 28 national parliaments and the EP ever concluding an inter- institutional agreement on anything other than exchange of information. AFCO adopted the report on 18 March. Whereas Casini had called for a more formal framework of rules and procedures for the 'interparliamentary system' to be established, MEPs backed the compromise wording which stated that any attempt to devise a common framework for interparliamentary cooperation at this stage would be premature.

The European Union: A Democratic Institution? 129

> The report recommended that COSAC should remain a forum for regular exchange of views, information and best practice, but that it could focus its discussions in particular on the general state of the integration process.
>
> MEPs rejected by one vote amendments which would have called on the Commission to provide more detailed subsidiarity justifications and to recognise that the current eight-week deadline for Reasoned Opinions was insufficient. They also rejected Casini's proposal for an inter- parliamentary agreement to be concluded between the EP and national parliaments which would form the basis for organised cooperation under Article 9 of the Protocol on the Role of National Parliaments.
>
> It recommended *inter alia* that the role of the EU Speakers' Conference in inter- parliamentary relations should be more clearly defined and placed on a more formal institutional footing, and that inter-parliamentary cooperation was welcome and should be open and inclusive. It concluded that the lack of transparency of Council deliberations makes it difficult for governments to be genuinely accountable to national parliaments.
>
> The report was debated in plenary on 14-17 April 2014.

The EP is perceived as reluctant to see any diminution of its powers or any form of cooperation with national parliaments that might impinge on its legislative role, yet it has called for more cooperation with national parliaments, in order to enhance its work and the work of multi-lateral assemblies such as the Inter-Parliamentary Union (IPU). EP Vice- President Miguel Angel Martinez told the Lords EU Committee: "We cannot simply increase the role of national parliaments if their role is seen as a way of attacking the Europea n Parliament or trying to undermine the way that European institutions work".[214]

Is there an inherent and fundamental conflict between the EP and national parliaments that will prevent them from forming a democratic partnership at the European and national levels? Raffaello Matarazzo[215] commented that since 1979 the two parliamentary levels have competed with, rather than complemented, each other:

> .... the NPs [national parliaments] and the EP continue to incorporate two opposing approaches to EU integration: the NPs tend to defend the inter-governmental dimension of the EU, considering the EP as an antagonist and possible threat, while the EP conceives its function as that of the main promoter of integration. Political dialogue between these actors will continue

to be undermined by this differing view: the entry into force of the new Treaty has, in fact, increased inter- institutional dialogue, but it has also enlarged the scope for competition, in particular the scrutiny of sensitive issues like CFSP and CSDP.[216]

5.6. A Separate Chamber for National Parliaments?

Menon's proposed solution to the EP legitimacy problem is simple but radical ("surgical", as he puts it): shut it down and let national parliaments perform its functions, thereby ensuring "adequate democratic scrutiny of all EU legislation" (assuming national parliaments *do* adequately scrutinise EU business – see above). Voting on EU matters could be done in national parliaments using electronic voting systems; it would save money (no need for the three EP seats in Brussels, Strasbourg and Luxembourg); and it would, in his view, "advance democratic legitimation. For entrusting national parliaments with legislative tasks at the European level would - at a stroke - serve to strengthen the union itself". Menon is pessimistic about the future of democratic reform in the EU without such a change:

> Europeans will have no option but to watch in dismay as, every five years, the EU itself is brought into disrepute by elections in which abstentions rise and nationally-inspired protest-votes send representatives to Brussels and Strasbourg with no real democratic mandate.[217]

In their 2010 report, Menon and Peet note the progress made by national parliaments in acquiring a role in EU politics and suggest four ways in which the EP and national parliaments could move forward.

- Set up a new body, like the United States Senate, that would represent national parliaments (like the German *Bundesrat*); floated in the 2001 *Laeken declaration*, but it is unlikely that the establishment of another EU institution would be supported with EU voters, and "a European senate could quickly find itself uselessly duplicating the work of the European Parliament" unless the latter were abolished - highly unlikely.
- Getting national parliaments more explicitly engaged in holding to account national governments in the Council. This proposal emphasises the importance of EU scrutiny committees in national

parliaments, of summoning ministers to appear before EU committees ahead of meetings, and of national EU committees working more closely together through COSAC to co-ordinate their positions. OR: national parliamentary committees appoint an EU rapporteur to look into European matters that fall within their competence. This would involve UK departmental select committees in looking at how national policy feeds into EU policy.

- National parliaments could insist on being consulted more explicitly over the choice of Commissioners. Although Commissioners are supposed to act collegially, "the notion that commissioners also in some way represent their countries has become widespread". National parliaments should therefore be able to debate and approve national governments' choices before the EP hearings.
- National parliaments and the EP should work more closely together, co-operating closely with their MEPs in joint investigations and big reports. "The cultures of Brussels, Strasbourg and national capitals might need to change to make this possible", but the main challenge would be for national MPs and MEPs to hold the Commission and national governments to account.[218]
- In a Commons debate on 16 July 2013 on national parliaments and the EU, the European Scrutiny Committee Chair, Bill Cash, was critical of institutional duplication, which he called "completely unworkable".[219]

6. UK GOVERNMENT AND PARLIAMENTARY VIEWS

6.1. Introduction

For the current Conservative-led UK Government, democracy remains fundamentally rooted in the state, and international cooperation should therefore be primarily intergovernmental in nature. The Conservative Party election manifesto in 2010 stated: "We believe Britain's interests are best served by membership of a European Union that is an association of its Member States. We will never allow Britain to slide into a federal Europe ". It promised to seek negotiations to "return powers that we believe should reside with the UK, not the EU" (repatriation of EU powers).

The Foreign Secretary William Hague outlined why, in his view, giving the EP more powers had not remedied the democratic deficit, and how national parliaments could do so:

> The European Parliament has an important role that is set out in the treaties and many MEPs do excellent work. However, over the past 20 years, member states have granted the European Parliament a dramatic increase in its powers through successive treaties, in the hope that it would address the growing sense of distance and disengagement among European voters. That manifestly has not worked. The question of democratic disconnection and accountability has not gone away. That suggests that we need a different answer. That answer will include a bigger and more significant role for national Parliaments, which are and will remain the true the source of democratic legitimacy in the European Union. By according a greater role to national Parliaments, we will give practical effect and real force to the principle of subsidiarity.[220]

Several UK initiatives to tackle democracy and legitimacy issues are underway or have recently been completed:

- ***European Union Act 2011*** allows the UK Parliament to mandate the Government not to agree to the adoption of certain measures in the Council unless they have been approved by an Act of Parliament and in some cases a referendum.[221]
- **Review of the Balance of Competences** The Government's ***Review of the Balance of Competences*** is due to conclude in autumn 2014. The Review aims to deepen understanding of the UK's EU membership and provide a constructive contribution to the wider European debate about modernising, reforming and improving the EU. The Review will help inform the Government for its proposed renegotiation of the EU Treaties.[222]
- **European Scrutiny Committee report on scrutiny of the EU** On 28 November 2013 the Commons European Scrutiny Committee published Reforming the European Scrutiny System in the House of Commons.[223] See below for conclusions.
- **House of Lords report on the role of national parliaments** The House of Lords European Union Committee published its report on the Role of National Parliaments in the European Union on 24 March 2014.

The European Union: A Democratic Institution? 133

- **Fresh Start Project** The Fresh Start Project involving MPs across party lines, think tanks, interest groups, Peers, MEPs and constitutional experts, is looking at options for a new UK -EU relationship.

6.2. Bloomberg Speech

In his Bloomberg speech on 23 January 2013, the Prime Minister pledged that the Conservative election manifesto in 2015 would "ask for a mandate from the British people for a Conservative government to negotiate a new settlement with our European partners in the next Parliament..". This would be followed by a referendum in the first half of the next Parliament (i.e. by the end of 2017) on whether to stay in the EU on the new terms, or leave altogether.

David Cameron explained that as an "island nation", Britain had a distinctive character and view of Europe, but was not "un-European". The five principles for his "vision for a new European Union, fit for the 21st Century" were:

> "My fourth principle is democratic account-ability: we need to have a bigger and more significant role for national parliaments.
> … It is national parliaments, which are, and will remain, the true source of real democratic legitimacy and accountability in the EU".
>
> David Cameron, 'Bloomberg speech', 23 January 2013

- Competitiveness: "creating a leaner, less bureaucratic Union, relentlessly focused on helping its member countries to compete";
- Flexibility: "We need a structure that can accommodate the diversity of its members— North, South, East, West, large, small, old and new. Some of whom are contemplating much closer economic and political integration. And many others, including Britain, who would never embrace that goal";
- Power back to Members: "power must be able to flow back to Member States, not just away from them";
- Democratic accountability: "we need to have a bigger and more significant role for national parliaments. There is not, in my view, a single European demos. It is national parliaments, which are, and will

remain, the true source of real democratic legitimacy and accountability in the EU";

- Fairness: "whatever new arrangements are enacted for the Eurozone, they must work fairly for those inside it and out".

In written evidence to the Lords EU Committee inquiry in September 2013, David Lidington outlined two ways in which to tackle the EU's democracy challenge: by increasing the role of national democracies through the Council and European Council, "and for national parliaments to play a greater and more effective role in the EU's functioning". As to why national parliaments should have a role in the EU framework, he said that "people in Europe identify with their national parliaments more than with EU institutions. They understand how to make their voice heard through national parliaments. National parliaments are closer to, and understand better, the concerns of citizens". The Government, he said, was discussing the following matters with EU partners:

- Increased coordination between national parliaments, possibly by strengthening existing cooperation channels, particularly COSAC, and establishing new channels (joint committee meetings, or regular evidence sessions from Commissioners or MEPs).
- Earlier and more direct engagement by national parliaments with EU institutions. The Government would encourage Parliament to consider increasing its level of representation in Brussels (other States' chambers have 10-20 staff; the UK has three).
- Changes to the processes in Brussels: more effective use of yellow and orange cards; identify earlier Commission proposals which raise subsidiarity concerns, including through better analysis of subsidiarity implications in Commission legislative proposals. Making it easier for national parliaments to challenge EU legislation: e.g. strengthening existing yellow card process (giving parliaments more time, lowering the threshold of the number of parliaments required to trigger a yellow card, extending scope of the card e.g. to cover proportionality); perhaps allowing national parliaments working together the power to force the Commission to withdraw a proposal ('red card' procedure).
- We should explore whether such cards might be issued at any point during the legislative process and indeed whether they could be exercised in relation to existing legislation. The Government would also support a number of COSAC's recommendations, including that the Commission should make a political commitment that it will respond to opinions or requests issued by more than a third of chambers. And the Government is interested in Parliament's views on whether national parliaments working through COSAC might issue "own initiative"

The European Union: A Democratic Institution? 135

reports, emulating in part the European Parliament's practice, in order to enhance the political dialogue process. Such changes could be achieved through political agreement between Member States and the EU institutions in the short term, and/or through any future Treaty change.

6.3. A National Veto Mechanism: Proposals for a 'Red Card' Mechanism

The Lisbon Treaty innovations on the role of national parliaments, although welcomed by the UK Government, did not go far enough to satisfy David Cameron's conviction that national parliaments are the true source of real democratic legitimacy and accountability in the EU.[224]

David Lidington told the Lords EU Committee inquiry in September 2013:

> We want to make more effective use of the existing yellow and orange cards and identify earlier Commission proposals which raise subsidiarity concerns. In addition, we want to make it easier for national parliaments to challenge EU legislation. For example, we should consider strengthening the existing yellow card process (giving parliaments more time, lowering the threshold of the number of parliaments required to trigger a yellow card, and extending the scope of the card e.g. to cover proportionality), and consider proposals to give national parliaments working together the power to force the Commission to withdraw a proposal (a 'red card' procedure). We should explore whether such cards might be issued at any point during the legislative process and indeed whether they could be exercised in relation to existing legislation. The Government would also support a number of COSAC's recommendations, including that the Commission should make a political commitment that it will respond to opinions or requests issued by more than a third of chambers.

The current subsidiarity mechanism is a means of engaging in political dialogue with the EU institutions, rather than a means of blocking unwanted EU legislation. UK views include both strengthening the current subsidiarity early warning (yellow card) system and introducing a 'red card' veto. When, during the negotiations on the *Treaty Establishing a Constitution for Europe*, the UK Labour MP Gisela Stuart suggested a red card mechanism that would be triggered by a two-thirds threshold, it was rejected by the IGC (and later by the Lisbon Treaty IGC) on the grounds that it might undermine the Commission's right of initiative and slow down the legislative process with national vetoes. On the other hand, as the Lords EU Committee noted in its 11th Report of 2002-3: "This can be countered by the argument that a two-thirds threshold is going to be quite hard to achieve, meaning that the 'red card' will always remain a weapon of last resort". The Lords Committee concluded that the yellow card procedure would "in most circumstances, strike the right balance, providing an individual right to be heard, rather than a collective right to block". However, it recommended keeping the red card proposal:

> The successful marshalling of the necessary majority to activate the "red card" will, in our view, be a very rare event. The fact that so many national parliaments were concerned about a proposal might well reveal a serious concern that would need addressing. Any effective early warning system would of course require an effective mechanism to allow national parliaments to exchange information.

The Lisbon Treaty did not provide a blocking 'red card' mechanism, but since 2009 calls for a national veto power have increased – and not just from the UK Government. At the Königswinter Conference on 31 May 2013 William Hague spoke about a "crisis of legitimacy" that was undermining EU institutions, and called for national parliaments to be able to overrule Commission legislative proposals by means of a 'red card' system. This would "give national parliaments the right to block legislation that need not be agreed at the European level". As with the current 'yellow card' system, a minimum number of national parliaments would have to agree that the proposal should not be made by the EU. Hague also hailed 'enhanced cooperation' (whereby some Member States proceed with integration measures ahead of others) as evidence of a more flexible form of integration involving only Sta tes that wanted to integrate, and said that "ultimately the EU remains an inclusive club based on the four freedoms and the Single Market". He told the conference the UK wanted to help "make the EU more democratically responsive", solve the problem of the EU's lack of "mechanisms to decentralise – to push powers down as well as up", without which the EU would not be "democratically sustainable".

In evidence to the ESC on 4 July 2013, David Lidington outlined Government thinking on how to improve the EU's democratic legitimacy, starting with a repudiation of the view that giving the EP more powers would improve the situation, and going on to discuss a pos sible 'red card':

The European Union: A Democratic Institution? 137

Even before we get to the red card, there is a question about whether the yellow card procedure could be strengthened by looking again at the threshold and the scope of the yellow card process, which at the moment is limited to subsidiarity grounds but could be made wider to cover proportionality, disproportionate cost, the time given to national parliaments to put forward a reasoned opinion, or other grounds. But we thought it was right to bring forward the idea that we should go beyond the yellow card and propose an outright power of veto. If a given number of national parliaments around the EU said that a certain Commission proposal should be blocked, the Commission simply would not be able to review it and decide to resubmit but would have to take it off the table. It is not something the British Government have yet formally adopted as a policy, but it is an idea we have put out that we think needs serious consideration.

In November 2013 the Fresh Start Project outlined proposals for a red card procedure to be introduced via Treaty change, which would mean national parliaments could "combine to permanently block Commission proposals" and, more controversially, could seek to apply the red card to existing EU legislation. The group also suggested strengthening the existing yellow card system "by lowering the threshold for issuance and giving Parliaments more time to scrutinise proposals". In their view, the trigger for a subsidiarity notification to the Commission should be three national parliaments submitting reasoned opinions, rather than the current one third of national parliament votes, and "a significantly extended period for scrutiny" rather than the present eight weeks.[225]

David Lidington proposed that the red card might take the form of a "political commitment", (reminiscent of the earlier Luxembourg and Ioannina Compromises):

...we could make an advance ahead of reopening the treaties if the Commission were to say, "We agree that, once a given number of national Parliaments deploy a reasoned opinion against a proposal, we will treat that as an effective veto. We promise, as a matter of political commitment, that we will withdraw such a proposal." We could get a change of working practice at political level ahead of codifying it through treaty change.[226]

The European Scrutiny Committee Report on reforming EU scrutiny proposed more effective Government accountability, and more engagement on the Floor of the House, including specific EU questions, more engagement in EU matters in departmental select committees and a permanent membership of the ESC, rather than the current ad hoc, subject-based membership. There were also some radical proposals: the Committee emphasised the supremacy of the Westminster Parliament and proposed a national veto and the unilateral repeal of EU legislation. It recommended that "there should be a mechanism whereby the House of Commons can decide that a particular legislative proposal should not apply to the UK"; further, that "parallel provision should be made to enable a decision of the House of Commons to disapply parts of the existing acquis". This would require "an Act of Parliament to disapply the European Communities Act (1972) in relation to specific EU legislation".[227]

A letter from around a hundred Conservative MPs (about 17% of the Commons)[228] called on David Cameron to introduce a national veto of existing unwanted EU legislation, but, as William Hague pointed out in an interview on *Sky News* on 12 January 2014:

> ... if national parliaments all around the European Union were regularly and unilaterally able to choose which bits of EU they would apply and which bits they wouldn't, well then the European single market wouldn't work and indeed even a Swiss style arrangement, free trade arrangement with the European Union wouldn't work. So we have to be realistic about these things but we are working for more national accountability and we are finding common cause with other people in Europe such as in the Netherlands for instance, on some of these ideas.

The Justice Secretary Chris Grayling told the BBC *Sunday Politics* show on 12 January 2014 that there could not be a situation "where one parliament could prevent laws happening across the whole of the European Union".

There are some obvious problems with a national veto of existing EU laws. EU law has primacy over national law, as confirmed by the Court of Justice and stated in the Treaty Declaration (see Section 2.4). Furthermore, the TFEU states in Article 288 that its legislative instruments are all binding and regulations "directly applicable in all Member States". As the Court of Justice concluded in *Flaminio Costa v E.N.E.L.* in 1964, this would become meaningless if a Member State could unilaterally nullify their effects by means of a contrary domestic legislative measure. The Court ruled that "The transfer by the states from their domestic legal system to the Community legal system of the rights and obligations arising under the treaty carries with it a permanent limitation of their sovereign rights, against which a subsequent unilateral act incompatible with the concept of the Community cannot prevail".

The European Union: A Democratic Institution? 139

Support for a 'Red Card' in the EU?

According to *Open Europe*'s ComRes poll, 22-24 May 2013, one of the top four priorities for a renegotiation of the UK's EU membership was "giving the UK parliament more powers to block unwanted EU laws". A red card is also supported by *Business for Britain*. It is hard to assess the level of support among other EU governments for a red card procedu re. In 2007, when the Lisbon Treaty was being negotiated, Poland, the Czech Republic and the Netherlands supported such a procedure.[229] According to an *Open Europe* report in September 2011, "European localism" would be supported by Scandinavia, the Netherlan ds, most of Eastern Europe and the German Länder.[230]

The Dutch Government appears to be a firm supporter of strengthened subsidiarity. In a review of subsidiarity and proportionality in June 2013, it called for "a more sober but more effective EU, starting from the principle: 'at European level only when necessary, at national level whenever possible'".[231] The Dutch Government argued that power and responsibility should be at local, national, European, or global level, depending on the issue. It stated that the "time of an ever- closer union in every possible policy area is behind us", preferring the principle of "Europe where necessary, national where possible". In a speech on 30 October 2013 the Dutch Prime Minister, Mark Rutte, echoed much of what the Fresh Start Group and the Government have been saying about looking at which tasks are better performed by Member States, and which by Europe. The Dutch Foreign Minister, Frans Timmermans, wrote in a *Financial Times* article, Monnet's Europe needs reform to fit the 21st century, on 14 November 2013:

> ... we would encourage national parliaments to bring Europe back home where it belongs and strengthen their co-operation with each other and the European parliament. They should have the right to summon commissioners to capitals. And if one-third of national parliaments raise subsidiarity objections to a legislative proposal (the yellow card procedure), the commission should not just reconsider, it should use its discretion to take the disputed proposal off the table, turning the yellow card into a red.

According to a report by Rem Korteweg of the *Centre for European Reform*, the Dutch subsidiarity review has received support from Germany, Sweden, Finland and Austria, and even the EP President, Martin Schulz.[232] However, the author did not think the Dutch Government would support David Cameron in his quest for "radical changes to the EU", and the 2013 *Tweede*

Kamer report on national parliaments in the EU did not call for a red card system.

Before the 2013 German election Chancellor Merkel was reported as wanting more direct agreements between EU Member States - an intergovernmental rather than an EU approach - and during her election campaign, she was widely reported as saying she saw "no need to give more authority to Brussels". Open Europe reported on 31 May 2013 on a guest piece in the *Frankfurter Allgemeine Zeitung,* 31 May 2013, by Professor Dr. Hans Hugo Klein, a former CDU MP and judge at the German Constitutional Court. He argued that "the principle of subsidiarity needs to be defined in more detail" followed by a "thorough check of existing EU law", and that, in order not to alienate the people in Europe, "a repatriation of EU competences and a thinning-out of European rules and regulations is required".

Opinion polls show a fall in public support for the EU and more support for domestic decision-making, Jose Ignacio Torreblanca (European Council on Foreign Relations) reported on 1 October 2013. He noted a poll in May 2007 in which 57% of Germans tended to trust the EU, compared with only 29% in the *Eurobarometer* spring 2013 poll. Data collected in August 2013 for a *YouGov Deutschland* poll for Open Europe and Open Europe Berlin seem to confirm this trend: 60% of voters thought national parliaments should be given more powers to block unwanted EU laws (25% disagreed).

CONCLUSION

There is talk of another EU Treaty reform - not just by UK Government, but by the EU institutions and other Member States. Commission President Barroso has called for a "deep and genuine economic union, based on political union", while Council President Van Rompuy has tried to strengthen Eurozone governance within the existing Treaty framework.

But what is actually on the reform agenda? Will it stand a chance of being adopted and if so, will it make the EU more democratic? The last reform process lasted eight years from the Laeken Declaration to the Lisbon Treaty, yet for many the democratic deficit, particularly since the euro crisis, appears to have deepened. In a speech on 7 January 2014, Commission Vice President Viviane Reding spoke of making the EU more democratic and transparent by creating a "United States of Europe with the Commission as government and two chambers – the European Parliament and a 'Senate' of Member States".

The European Union: A Democratic Institution? 141

She called for a broad debate on the future of Europe before the "required" changes are made.

For some, including the UK Government, the way forward is to allow Member States to loosen the EU framework in more policy areas and thereby to preserve national sovereignty.[233] National parliaments have democratic legitimacy at the national level; this needs to be transferred onto the EU stage so that they can become actors there. The European Scrutiny Committee suggestions234 and the letter from Conservative MPs to David Cameron in January 2014 take this further: the re-establishment of a national veto of EU proposals, which would not only "transform the UK's negotiating position in the EU", but transform the negotiating position of the other 27 Member States.

What can be done about the falling support for the EU as an institution among the electorates of Europe? If the EU has a *demos* (the UK Government and the German Constitutional Court argue that it does not), it still fails to attract trust or even interest among its citizens. Its institutions lack transparency, and all too often their deliberations and decisions are subject to the 'black market' scrutiny of the tabloid press, sometimes long before national parliaments have scrutinised them.

What are the chances of a radical Treaty amendment that would suit the current UK Government? Roger Liddle comment in *The Europe Dilemma: Britain and the Drama of EU Integration* that "Views on the likelihood of a process of full-blown treaty change have waxed and waned".[235] The assumed timetable of a Treaty amendment process being launched after the EP elections, a convention in 2015-16 and an IGC in 2016-17, would, as Liddle points out, be compatible with the David Cameron's timetable, but would it achieve the ambitious reforms the UK Government seeks before putting UK membership of the EU to a referendum?

The Foreign Office Minister, Lord Howell, in a debate on 9 January 2014, thought the UK Government was gathering support for wide-scale EU reform – even if their ideas of reform were different from the UK's – and he listed a number of other reform-minded Member States (Poland, the Netherlands, Sweden, the Czech Republic, Slovakia, Hungary, the Baltic and Mediterranean States). But he made clear that "It must be European reform, not just reform of the narrow issue of Britain's relations with the rest of the European Union". In Germany, says Liddle, "In principle, the Christian Democratic Union … supports a radical leap forward in political integration, creating a federal European finance ministry, and a directly elected EU president", but Chancellor Merkel is cautious, and therefore he thinks, "if there is German backing for treaty change, it will be limited in scope".[236]

Some observers think the EU has reached a critical point in its evolution, a point at which a radical change could, or should, be made. John Wyles, writing in *European Voice* in January 2014 about the dwindling public support for the EU and its institutions, thought this offered "nothing but encouragement for those who dream of strict curbs on 'Brussels' or even of taking their countries out of the Union".[237] Governments were, he wrote, "gradually and almost imperceptibly ... adopting a crablike shuffle away from the model of political and economic integration that has ruled for most of the last 60 years". Predicting successes for eurosceptics in the EP elections, Wyles thinks governments "will have to take a fresh look at the balance of competences between the Union and its member countries. And a revision through subsequent treaty changes could be equally unavoidable".

Not all institutional reform requires Treaty amendment. The Lords EU Committee concluded that there was ample scope for institutional reform without Treaty amendment:

> Treaty change is not necessary to enhance the role of national parliaments in the EU: substantial improvements can, and should, be achieved without treaty change. To a significant degree it is a matter for the will of parliamentarians to insist on securing substantial and lasting changes, and of their governments to give effect to that will. Important improvements could be achieved through the autonomous action of national parliaments, and through actions collectively agreed between the national parliaments, the Commission, the Council and the European Parliament where relevant. This report sets out options for reforms which could be pursued in such agreements.

Robert Howse and Kalypso Nicolaidis have written of the "largely impossible nature of the task of squaring the federalist idea with the modern statist conception of sovereignty".[238] If democracy is fundamentally rooted in the state, Reding's proposal for more democracy along with more integration, has an inescapable - if for the UK Government unpalatable - logic: should not the EU, to make it more democratic, legitimate and accountable, be given the structures and institutions of a democratic, legitimate and accountable state? On the other hand, while the hybrid model encompassing intergovernmental, EU and differentiated arrangements, is creaky, it has nevertheless survived for over 50 years. Treaty changes have allowed the EU to expand and change, patching up weaknesses, but also making it more flexible and adaptable to the demands of its growing and diverse membership. The Lisbon Treaty reforms did not radically change the EU's institutional structure. Laurent Pech commented that EU governments were "motivated by two somewhat contradictory impulses when devising the [Lisbon Treaty]: They wanted to make the EU more democratic and efficient whilst avoiding any process of state-building".[239] With any future changes, can the dynamic of EU political and economic integration, efficiency and democratic legitimacy be reconciled with the preservation of Member State sovereignty, national vetoes and opt-outs?

The debate continues.

APPENDIX GERMAN CONSTITUTIONAL COURT RULING ON LISBON TREATY

German Constitutional Court Ruling on the Lisbon Treaty – Is the EP an Institution of EU Democracy?

In pre-Maastricht debates in the early 1990s, the German *Bundestag* called for the EU's democratic deficit to be eliminated, in particular by strengthening the EP's legislative powers. The German Constitutional Court ruling on the *Maastricht Treaty* on 12 October 1993 argued that, having no demos, European democracy had to be based on "... the existence of specific privileged conditions, such as ongoing free interaction of social forces, interests, and ideas, in the course of which political objectives are also clarified and modified, and as a result of which public opinion moulds political policy". The Court also ruled that national legislative bodies were the relevant organs to convey democratic legitimacy in the context of Germany's participation in the process of European integration.

During the Amsterdam Intergovernmental Conference which gave rise to the *Amsterdam Treaty* the *Bundestag* supported the EP in becoming a co-legislator with the Council, rather than supporting a stronger role for national parliaments in the legislative process. Subsequently, the German Parliament insisted on, and received from the Government, its own right to approve EU matters.

In a ruling in June 2009 on the compatibility of the Lisbon Treaty with the German Constitution (Lisbon Case, BVerfG, 2 BvE 2/08, 30 June 2009), the Constitutional Court refused to endorse the EP as a primary institution of EU democracy. In ruling on the constitutionality of various Treaty reforms, the Court formulated a "democracy *solange*" (as long as), establishing the extent to which the EU can develop as a constitutional and legal entity. In the ruling the Court raised interesting arguments about the nature of the EU and its lack of a 'demos', concluding that the EP does not represent the EU people because the EU does not have a 'people'. It placed the national parliaments of the Member States ahead of the EP, as long as ("solange") the Union continues to be founded on the principle of conferral – i.e. the Member States confer power on the EU to act and the EU itself has no general power to decide its own powers (*Kompetenz-Kompetenz*). The Court used this argument to support German approval of the Treaty. The principle of 'conferral', the Court argued, secures democratic legitimacy in the EU. Without this principle the EU could exercise both the powers conferred on it by the Member States and also those created by the EU; the EU would be able to decide its own powers and would therefore exhibit the characteristics of a state. The Court emphasised that the EU is not a state, but an association of States (*Staatenberbund*); and the EP is not "a body of representation of a sovereign European people", but "a supranational body of representation of the peoples of the Member States, so that the principle of electoral equality, which is common to all European states, is not applicable with regard to the European Parliament". The ruling continued:

> Other provisions of the Treaty of Lisbon, such as the double qualified majority in the Council (Article 16.4 TEU Lisbon, Article 238.2 of the Treaty on the Functioning of the European Union), the elements of participative, associative and direct democracy (Art. 11
> TEU Lisbon) as well as the institutional recognition of the national Parliaments (Article 12 TEU Lisbon) cannot compensate the deficit of European public authority that exists when measured against requirements on democracy in states, but can nevertheless increase the level of legitimisation of the *Staatenverbund*.

In the Lisbon judgment the Court turned the legitimacy argument on its head: it assumed that parliamentary democracy exists *only* in the Member States, and that, as the EU is not a state with a sovereign people, but an association of states, the EU cannot and need not fulfil the national criteria for a democracy. The election of Members of the German *Bundestag* by the people fulfils its central role in the system of the federal and supranational intertwining of power "only if the *Bundestag*, which represents the people, and the Federal Government sustained by it, retain a formative influence on the political development in Germany. This is the case if the German *Bundestag*

The European Union: A Democratic Institution? 145

retains responsibilities and competences of substantial political importance or if the Federal Government, which is answerable to it politically, is in a position to exert a decisive influence on European decision-making procedures".

Professor Davor Jancic noted that Germany's Lisbon judgement represented the climax of the "emphasis on the democratic legitimization of the European Union by national parliaments" and "In the "democracy solange," the [Constitutional Court] denied the possibility for the European Parliament ever to surpass its supplementary character".

Source: *Columbia Journal of European Law*, Vol. 16 (3), 2010; LSE Research online, August 2013. For further information on the *solange* judgments, see Davor Jancic, "Caveats from Karlsruhe and Berlin: whither democracy after Lisbon?" 2010; LSE Research online, August 2013.

End Notes

[1] A. Bullock and O. Stallybrass eds, *Fontana Dictionary of Modern Thought* (7th edition, London,1981)

[2] Andrew Heywood, *Politics* (Basingstoke, 2002), p69

[3] One version of representative democracy breaks with the majoritarian approach to decision-making. Consociational democracy, under which power is shared between elected representatives of all the main social groups in a country, has sometimes been introduced in post-conflict societies where it is feared a majoritarian approach to decision-making could trigger renewed violence. Past and present examples include Lebanon, Burundi and Northern Ireland.

[4] In his famous book *Democracy in America* (New York, 1945 [first published in 1835]), Alexis de Tocqueville argued that the web of voluntary associations and intermediate institutions existing in the early United States helped to prevent its democracy degenerating into a "tyranny of the majority". For a more recent advocate of the positive case, see E.Olin Wright, *Envisioning Real Utopias* (London, 2010), pp152-53

[5] Heywood, p81

[6] R. Williams, *Keywords* (London, 1983), p93

[7] Ibid, p94

[8] See, for example: D. Reuschemeyer, E. Stephens and J. Stephens. *Capitalist Development and Democracy* (Cambridge, 1992)

[9] Bullock and Stallybrass

[10] Heywood, p77. The Nazi regime in Germany operated on a similar basis between the 1920s and 1945, leading Hannah Arendt after the Second World War to coin the concept of totalitarianism to describe what Nazism and Stalinism had in common.

[11] Heywood, p77

[12] B. Brivati, J. Buxton and A. Selsdon, *The Contemporary History Handbook* (Manchester, 1996), pp43-46

[13] For a concise exposition of this argument, see: D. Harvey, *A Brief History of Neoliberalism* (Oxford, 2007)

[14] M. Woolf, "The big questions raised by anti-capitalist protests", *www.ft.com*, 27 October 2011

[15] Another way of describing these checks and balances is the separation of powers. For example, see Library Standard Note 6503, "The separation of powers" (last updated 16 August 2011)

[16] The relationship between democracy and power has been a major preoccupation of political theorists over the decade. See, for example: B. Barry, *Democracy, Power and Justice: Essays in Political Theory* (Oxford, 1989)

[17] Heywood, p70

[18] "Accountability and transparency: essential principles", www.democracyweb.org

[19] "Political legitimacy", Stanford Encyclopaedia of Philosophy, last updated April 2010

[20] A related formulation is "constitutional sovereignty", which is often used in the context of the sovereignty of parliament For example, see H.L.A. Hart, *The Concept of Law* (Oxford, 1994), pp149-50

[21] For the sake of simplicity, the use here of the term 'state' should be taken to include the term 'nation-state'.

[22] S. Besson, "Sovereignty", *Max Planck Encyclopedia of Public International Law*, para 72 [last updated April 2011 – available on request from the Library]

[23] Besson, "Sovereignty", paras 70-71

[24] Besson, "Sovereignty", para 131

[25] Products of this trend include the International Criminal Court and the international legal norm known as 'The Responsibility to Protect'.

[26] L. Whitehead, "State sovereignty and democracy: an awkward coupling", in P. Burnell and R. Youngs, *New Challenges to Democratization* (Abingdon and New York, 2010), pp30-32

[27] See, for example, P. Oborne, *The Triumph of the Political Class* (London, 2007) and G. Allen, *Reinventing Democracy* (London, 1995)

[28] For a discussion of these issues and more, see "The state of accountability in 2013", Centre for Public Scrutiny, 2013

[29] Many analysts would argue that today it is large corporations – not least those which specialise in providing public services through contracts with the state – which embody this problem. See, for example: D. Beetham, "Unelected Oligarchy: Corporate and Financial Dominance in Britain's Democracy", Democratic Audit UK, 2011

[30] See Library Standard Note 5125, "Membership of UK political parties" (last updated 3 December 2012); "Voter turnout in Western Europe since 1945", International IDEA, 2004

[31] The power to recall MPs has been on the political agenda in the UK. "Recall of MPs", www.gov.uk (last updated 29 November 2013)

[32] Occupy is perhaps the most prominent example or recent years. See, for example: D. Graeber, *The Democracy Project: a History, a Crisis, a Movement* (London, 2013)

[33] For one discussion of these issues, see V. Sperling, *Altered States. The Globalization of Accountability* (Cambridge, 2009)

[34] For a discussion of some of these issues, see: T. Zweifel, *International Organizations and Democracy: Accountability, Politics, and Power* (Boulder, 2005)

[35] For example, A. Stutzer and B. Frey, "Making international organisations more democratic", *Review of Law & Economics*, January 2013.

[36] L. Martell, "Cosmopolitanism and global politics", *Political Quarterly*, Autumn 2011

[37] J. Ingram, *Radical Cosmopolitics: The Ethics and Politics of Democratic Universalism* (New York, 2013). Sceptics might replace the word 'radical' with 'populist'.

[38] See, for example, E.Olin Wright, *Envisioning Real Utopias* (London, 2010)

[39] Dr Gavin Barrett, University College Dublin, Written evidence to House of Lords EU Committee, The Role of National Parliaments in the European Union, 6 February 2014.

[40] Federal Constitutional Court Press office, Press release no. 72/2009 of 30 June 2009 (re. Judgment of 30 June 2009 on Act Approving the Treaty of Lisbon compatible with the Basic Law).

[41] EU Democratic Legitimacy and National Parliaments, CEPS essay No. 7, 25 November 2013

[42] "Democracy and the European Union", in *Developments in the European Union* edited by Laura Cram, Desmond Dinan and Neill Nugent, 1999

The European Union: A Democratic Institution? 147

[43] Director of the Luiss School of Government and Professor of Political Science and International Relations at LUISS Guido Carli

[44] *Presseurop*, 4 September 2013, "A third way forward for Europe"

[45] Michael Burgess is Professor of Federal Studies and Director of the Centre for Federal Studies (CFS)

[46] Michael Burgess, *Federalism and European Union: The building of Europe, 1950–2000*, 2000, p. 49.

[47] Hague Academy and New York University.

[48] Chapter 2, *Federalism without Constitutionalism: Europe's Sonderweg: the federal vision: legitimacy and levels of governance in the United States and the European Union*, "Europe has charted its own brand of constitutional federalism. It works. Why fix it?" 2003.

[49] Wallace, ibid.

[50] Laurent Pech, "The Institutional Development of the EU Post-Lisbon: A case of plus ça change…?" UCD Dublin European Institute Working Paper 11-5, December 2011.

[51] Helen Wallace, "Designing Institutions for an Enlarging European Union", *Ten Reflections on the Constitutional Treaty for Europe* edited by Bruno de Witte, European University Institute, 2003

[52] COM (2001) 428 final, 25 July 2001.

[53] Kenneth Armstrong, School and Department of Law, Queen Mary, University of London, called the claim a "half truth", noting that the EU had only recently acquired "the bells and whistles of democratic constitutionalism". He thought they had been the "product of transnational technocratic decision-making among élite political actors".

[54] See, for example, *Financial Times*, 16 June 2008, Gideon Rachman, Ireland's bold blow for democracy.

[55] See, for example, Case C-376/98, Germany v Parliament and Council (tobacco advertising), [2000] ECR I-8419.

[56] The word 'democracy' or 'democratic' is used 16 times in total in the EU Treaties, Protocols and Declarations, which number over 400 pages: 10 times in the TEU, twice in the TFEU, once in the Protocols, once in the Declarations and twice in the European Charter of Fundamental Rights.

[57] EU membership criteria require that the candidate countries must have achieved, amongst other things, stability of institutions guaranteeing democracy, the rule of law, human rights and respect for and protection of minorities.

[58] The principle set out in Article 5(3) TEU, whereby the EU should act only if action at EU level would be more effective than at national level.

[59] For more information on the protocols, see SN/IA/6297, 12 April 2012

[60] See, for example, Carlo Casini, Chair of the EP's Constitutional Affairs Committee, uncorrected evidence, Lords Select Committee on the European Union Inquiry on the Role of National Parliaments 9 January 2014.

[61] Lord Boswell of Aynho, Chair of Lords EU Committee, uncorrected evidence, 9 January 2014.

[62] See Standard Note 6871, Democratic Legitimacy and the EU: reading list, 29 April 2014.

[63] *Foreign Affairs*, Vol. 51 No. 4 July 1973, "The Community is Working"

[64] He was referring to the EEC in *Parliament for Europe*.

[65] See also, for example, *Journal of Common Market Studies*, 2006 Volume 44. Number 3. pp. 533–62, "Why There is a Democratic Deficit in the EU: A Response to Majone and Moravcsik", Andreas Follesdal (University of Oslo) and Simon Hix (London School of Economics).

[66] Under the early warning mechanism set out in the subsidiarity protocol, national parliaments have the right to challenge a Commission proposal on subsidiarity grounds, forcing the Commission to rethink but not necessarily revise or withdraw the proposal.

[67] EP Constitutional Affairs Committee (AFCO) debate on COSAC and the Inter-parliamentary Conference on Economic and Financial Governance, 16 December 2013.

[68] Trilogues are composed of 2-3 MEPs, a Deputy Permanent Representative, normally from the State holding the EU Presidency, and a senior Commission official. The trilogue is a forum where each side in an OLP procedure can explain its position to the other and if possible say where agreement can be reached. The increase in trilogues may have implications for the balance of power between the institutions.

[69] Attempts to agree on common texts after a single reading, instead of going through second and even third readings. The Data Protection Package, Tobacco Products Directive, Clinical Trials Regulation and Medical Devices Regulations were all, controversially, agreed in this way. According to Lukas Obholzer and Christine Reh, first-reading agreements increased "from 28% in the 5th EP to 77% in the present legislative term". CEPS policy brief, How to Negotiate under Co-decision in the EU Reforming Trilogues and First-Reading Agreements, May 2012.

[70] The UN and Council of Europe, for example, have legal machinery which ensures compliance with convention obligations and which may impose sanctions for non-compliance.

[71] HC Deb Vol 831, 15.2.72, c282

[72] Professor of English Law, University of Oxford.

[73] *The European Constitution in the Making*, "The ECJ, National Courts and the Supremacy of Community Law",

[74] Regent's University London, The UK & Europe: Costs, Benefits, Options. The Regent's Report 2013, "The debate about Sovereignty" p.232.

[75] E.g. New article 23 on the European Union was introduced into the German Basic Law. A constitutional revision of 25 June 1992 gave the French Constitution Title XV to take account of Maastricht.

[76] Letter 14 December 1960

[77] [2003] QB 151

[78] Supreme Court, Queen's Bench Division, Divisional Court, 18 February 2002, Lord Justice Laws and Mr Justice Crane, at http://www.metricmartyrs.sageweb.co.uk/appealjudgment.htm

[79] http://www.hmcourts-service.gov.uk/judgmentsfiles/j1008/THOBURN_v_SUNDERLAND.htm

[80] Individuals can immediately invoke EU law before courts, independent of whether it has been enacted in national law. See Case 26/62, *Van Gend en Loos v Netherlands administratie der belastigen*.

[81] Case 6/64, *Costa v ENEL*; Case 41/74, *Van Duyn v Home Office*.

[82] See, for example, cases C-420/05P and C-415/05P, *Kadi* and *Al Barakaat*, Grand Chamber judgment, 3 September 2008, paras. 285 and 306-09.

[83] For example, in the *Arcelor* decision of 8 February 2007, the French *Conseil d'Etat* confirmed the supremacy of French constitutional law over international and EU law, while emphasising that the higher authority of the domestic constitution and the control of the constitutionality of EU acts by French judges must be reconciled with France's EU membership under Article 88-1 of the Constitution. The German Constitutional Court affirmed in *Görgülü* in 2004 that the Constitution (Basic Law) "does not waive the sovereignty contained in the last instance in the German constitution". See also German Constitutional Court Maastricht decision of 1993, BVerfGE 89, 155 (1992); in judgment 64/91, 22 March 1991, *Asepesco*, Spanish Constitutional Court implies that national authorities are bound by Spanish Constitution when implementing EU law; Danish High Court Maastricht Judgment of 6 April 1998, para. 9.6; Irish Supreme Court, judgement of 19 December 1989, Society for the Protection of Unborn Children Ireland v. Grogan, [1990] ILRM 350, 361 (separate opinion Walsh J); Section 18 of the UK's *European Union Act 2011* confirms the sovereignty of the UK Parliament: "Status of EU law dependent on continuing statutory basis. "Directly applicable or directly effective EU law (i.e. the rights, powers, liabilities, obligations, restrictions, remedies and procedures referred to in section 2(1) of the European Communities Act 1972) falls to be recognised and available in law in

the United Kingdom only by virtue of that Act or where it is required to be recognised and available in law by virtue of any other Act".

[84] Professor of public law and international law, University of Heidelberg School of Law; Director of Heidelberg Max Planck Institute for Comparative Public Law and International Law.

[85] Armin von Bogdandy, "Pluralism, Direct Effect, and the Ultimate Say: On the Relationship Between International and Domestic Constitutional Law" (2008) 6 *Journal of International Constitutional Law*, pp 397-413.

[86] Department of Public International Law, State and Constitutional Law, University of Basel

[87] www.icl-journal.com Vol 3 3/2009, 170, Supremacy Lost: International Law Meets Domestic Constitutional Law

[88] According to Freedom House criteria, all EU States are rated 1/1 except for Croatia and Hungary with 1/2, Italy with 2/1, and Bulgaria, Greece, Latvia and Romania with 2/2. A paper by DEMOS in 2013 argued that some States are "backsliding" in this respect (e.g. censorship under Hungary's media law).

[89] Some bicameral EU legislatures have an upper house that is not directly elected: the National Council of Slovenia, for example, is represented by certain interest groups; the UK House of Lords is represented by non-elected and appointed members.

[90] Head of the Rule of Law Centre, Wissenschaftszentrum Berlin für Sozialforschung.

[91] Prof Dr Mattias Kumm, Constitutionalism and the Moral Point of Constitutional Pluralism: Institutional Civil Disobedience and Conscientious Objection, in Dickson/Eleftheriadis, Philosophical Foundations of EU Law, OUP, 2012

[92] *Notre Europe* study 89, The Power of Initiative of the European Commission: A Progressive Erosion? Paolo Ponzano, Costanza Hermanin and Daniela Corona, February 2012.

[93] See, for example, the United Nations Security Council, where from 1945 to the end of 2009, 215 resolutions on substantive issues were vetoed. A recent example is China and Russia, two of the permanent five SC members, vetoing a UNSC resolution threatening sanctions against Syria in July 2012.

[94] *European governance - A white paper*, COM/2001/0428 final, 12 October 2001

[95] Professor of Law, Newcastle Law School, *A Critical Introduction to European Law*, 3rd ed., 2009, p19

[96] EU Democratic Legitimacy and National Parliaments, CEPS essay No. 7, 25 November 2013

[97] Political Opposition and the European Union', *Government and Opposition* 10 January 2007

[98] COM/2012/777 final, 28 November 2012.

[99] See Barroso's 2013 State of the Union address.

[100] Technische Universität Darmstadt, Institute for Political Science.

[101] For example, a citizens' dialogue was held in London on 10 February 2014 to discuss what the EU should be doing to tackle the euro crisis, what rights should citizens of the EU have and what the EU of the future should look like. http://ec.europa.eu/debate-future-europe/citizens-dialogues/unitedkingdom/london/index_en.htm

[102] Democratic Participation? The Involvement of Citizens in Policy-making at the European Commission', Journal of Contemporary European Research. Volume 6, Issue 3, pp. 335-352. A recent example of citizen participation in an EU-wide debate is the *Assises de la Justice* 2013, a forum on EU justice policies, to which the Commission asked for contributions from anyone with an interest in the conference issues and more broadly on the future justice policy of the EU.

[103] Assistant Professor of European Integration, Utrecht School of Governance.

[104] *Presseurop*, Caught in a democratic tangle, 3 April 2013 RESEARCH PAPER 14/25

[105] See Simon Hix and Bjørn Høyland, Empowerment of the European Parliament, 2013

[106] Quoted in *Europarl* Towards a Single Parliament: the influence of the ECSC Common Assembly on the Treaties of Rome 1957 – 2007, 50th anniversary of the Treaties of Rome.

[107] Quoted in *Europarl*, Towards Direct Elections to the European Parliament, Paper written to mark the 30th anniversary of direct elections (June 1979), 2009.

[108] Uncorrected evidence, 8 January 2014

[109] Professor of European Politics and Foreign Affairs, Kings College, London.

[110] Europe editor, *The Economist*.

[111] *Centre for European Reform*, Beyond the European Parliament: Rethinking the EU's democratic legitimacy, December 2010

[112] Another issue is the need for MEPs to travel between three different locations (Strasbourg, Brussels and Luxembourg. A single seat in Brussels would cut travel expenses and enable MEPs to spend more time dealing with policy and legislation.

[113] *Notre Europe*, Policy Paper 105, 11 February 2014, Heading towards a European Federation: Europe's last chance.

[114] *Centre for European Reform*, Can national parliaments make the EU more legitimate? Charles Grant,10 June 2013

[115] This section was written by Steven Ayres. See also Standard Note 6865, Turnout trends, 1979-2009, 14 April 2014.

[116] OECD Better Life Index: civic engagement.

[117] Sources: European Parliament, Turnout at the European elections (1979-2009) at http://www.europarl.europa.eu/aboutparliament/en/000cdcd9d4/Turnout-(1979-2009).html and International Institute for Democracy and Electoral Assistance (International IDEA) at http://www.idea.int/vt/.

[118] See Standard note 5442, UK Public Opinion on the European Union 16 April 2012.

[119] See IDEA, "Compulsory Voting", 21 March 2012.

[120] http://www.idea.int/uid/index.cfm

[121] Source: Institute for Democracy and Electoral Assistance

[122] Source: Institute for Democracy and Electoral Assistance Unified Database

[123] http://ec.europa.eu/public_opinion/cf/step1.cfm

[124] The question was: "As far as European politics are concerned, that is matters related to the European Community, to what extent would you say that you are interested in them?"

[125] Source: Europe Barometer and European Parliament

[126] The question was: "On the whole, are you very satisfied, fairly satisfied, not very satisfied or not at all satisfied with the way democracy works in the EU?"

[127] The question was: "Generally speaking, do you think that your country's membership of the European Community is: a good thing; a bad thing; neither good or bad; don't know?"

[128] Europeans' Engagement in Participatory Democracy, March 2013.

[129] *Open Democracy*, The European parliament: problem, and solution, 5 June 2009.

[130] The European Parliament – more powerful, less legitimate? An outlook for the 7th term, CEPS Working Document No. 314, Julia De Clerck-Sachsse and Piotr Maciejkaczynski, May 2009.

[131] Germany, France, UK, Italy, Spain, Poland, Greece and Czech Republic.

[132] *European Voice*, 16 May 2013

[133] *Financial Times* 2 January 2014

[134] Associate Professor, Department of Political Science, Vrije Universiteit Amsterdam

[135] EPIN Working Paper 10, December 2003, Staging European Union democracy: discussion paper prepared for round table on a sustainable project for Europe.

[136] Vienna Institute for Advanced Studies.

[137] LSE blog, Low turnout in European Parliament elections is driven by the perception that the process is not rewarding enough for voters, 9 August 2012.

[138] Research Fellow, Max Planck Institute for Comparative Public Law and International Law, Heidelberg.

[139] *German Law Journal* Vol. 10 No. 8, 2010, The Lisbon Case: A Critical Summary, Christian Wohlfahrt.

[140] Similarly, Lisbon Treaty innovations such as providing citizens with the possibility to communicate their views directly and the citizens' initiative "can only have a

The European Union: A Democratic Institution? 151

complementary and not a central function when it comes to legitimising European public authority": Wohlfahrt ibid.

[141] *Open Democracy*, The European parliament: problem, and solution, Anand Menon, 5 June 2009.

[142] Irving S. Ribicoff Visiting Associate Professor of Law at Yale Law School.

[143] *Harvard International Law Journal* Vol. 52, Number 1, Winter 2011, "What if Europe Held an Election and No One Cared?".

[144] *Journal of Common Market Studies*, 2006 Vol 44 Number 3. pp. 533–62, Andreas Follesdal (University of Oslo) and Simon Hix (London School of Economics) "Why There is a Democratic Deficit in the EU: A Response to Majone and Moravcsik".

[145] European Union Document No. 7648/13 and EU document No. 7650/13

[146] Reforming the Treaty on European Union – the legal debate, "Betwixt and between: democracy and transparency in the governance of the European Union", T.M.C. Asser Institut, 1995.

[147] However, there is no public record of how governments voted in the 1970s, 1980s and early 1990s.

[148] See Standard Note 6646, Voting Behaviour in the EU Council, 23 May 2013.

[149] Diagram from Eur-Lex, The legal order of the EU; see also useful Step-by-step flow diagram of the OLP, USEU/FAS Hilde Brans

[150] *Europa*, Legislative procedures.

[151] Codecision and Conciliation: A Guide to how the Parliament co-legislates under the Treaty of Lisbon, January 2012

[152] This figure varies, depending on whether sub-sections of Articles are counted separately.

[153] Anne Elizabeth Stie, Co-decision – the panacea for EU democracy? ARENA report February 2010. Stie's thesis is an excellent analysis of co-decision in a deliberative democratic process.

[154] *Statewatch Analysis*, The democratic accountability of the EU's legislative approach, December 2011.

[155] "It's the EU, Stupid", 5 September 2011

[156] *ARENA report*, Co-decision – the panacea for EU democracy? February 2010. Stie's thesis is an excellent analysis of co-decision in a deliberative democratic process.

[157] Brigid Laffan, "The Treaty of Maastricht: Political Authority and Legitimacy", *The State of the European Community: The Maastricht Debates and Beyond* 1993

[158] See Research Paper 04/54, "The Extension of Qualified Majority Voting from the Treaty of Rome to the European Constitution", 7 July 2004 and Standard Note 4639, "Lisbon Treaty: decision-making by Qualified Majority Voting or Unanimity", 28 February 2008.

[159] Continental Shift: Safeguarding the UK's financial trade in a changing Europe,

[160] EP factsheet at http://www.europarl.europa.eu/factsheets/2_2_0_en.htm

[161] Dr. Annette Schrauwen, Europa Instituut, Amsterdam Centre for International Law, Law Faculty, Universiteit van Amsterdam. Paper presented at conference "After the first 50 years: the future of European law and policy, "The Future of EU Citizenship: corrosion of national citizenship", Birmingham, 2-4 July 2008, at http://papers.ssrn.com/sol3/papers.cfm?abstract_id=1375413.

[162] Schrauwen, ibid

[163] Ibid

[164] Democratic Self-Government in Europe: Domestic Solutions to the EU Legitimacy Crisis, 15 May 2013

[165] In January 2011 the EP's ALDE group suggested scrapping advisory bodies to save taxpayers' money, and on the grounds that it does not "contribute significantly to the democratic decision-making process and the transparent, smooth and efficient running of the Union" (ALDE Position Paper on EU budget post-2013).

[166] See EESC website at http://www.eesc.europa.eu/?i=portal.en.events-and-activities-participatory- democracy- prospects

[167] Dr Gunnar Beck, Ifo Institute Munich Seminar, 28 January 2013, Law as the Continuation of Politics by Other Means - the Unconstitutional ESM and the ECB's Unlawful Bond Buying Programme oder der Rechtsstaat als Schönwetterveranstaltung. While in March 2014 the German Constitutional Court rejected the bulk of complaints against the European Stability Mechanism (ESM), the Court recently asked the EU Court to clarify the interpretation of the ECB statute that would allow for an application of OMT. Based on the ECJ's advice, the German Court will rule on whether the German government or German institutions such as the Bundesbank are allowed to participate in enabling decisions made by the ECB.

[168] Head of research, European Foundation.

[169] *European Journal,* 5 March 2013

[170] *Financial Times,* 2 January 2014

[171] Roger Liddle, *The Europe Dilemma: Britain and the Drama of EU integration,* 2014, p.224.

[172] For information on Germany and the euro crisis, see Library Research Paper 13/73, Germany's 2013 election: shaping the future? 17 December 2013

[173] *Voxeu* Can we move beyond the Maastricht orthodoxy? László Andor, 16 December 2013

[174] Written evidence, 24 September 2013.

[175] 8th Report, 2013–14.

[176] Evidence to European Scrutiny Committee, 12 June 2013

[177] HC Deb 16 July 2013, c 180WH

[178] Professor of Politics and International Affairs and Director, European Union Program, Princeton University.

[179] Cited in *CEPS* Working Document No. 286, February 2008, Democracy in the European Union

[180] A point also made by Bogdanor (2007), Hix (1999) and Schmitter (2000).

[181] Director General of *Assonime,* Professor at the College of Europe and Board Member of Centre for European Policy Studies (CEPS).

[182] Democracy in the European Union, CEPS Working Document No. 286/February 2008.

[183] Simon Hix and Andreas Follesdal, "Why there is a Democratic Deficit in the EU: a Response to Majone and Moravcsik", 2006, http://is.muni.cz/el/1423/podzim2013/EVS447/um/Presentation_6_Follesdal_Hix.txt.

[184] *CER,* Can national parliaments make the EU more legitimate? 10 June 2013.

[185] Final Report of the Future of Europe Group, 17 September 2012.

[186] Democratic Self-Government in Europe: Domestic Solutions to the EU Legitimacy Crisis, 15 May 2013. There is a response to Chalmers' suggestions in Killing the EU rather than quitting it, Olivier Rozenberg, Policy Network, 10 October 2013.

[187] See Standard Note 4462, EU Treaty Opt-ins and Opt-outs, 8 October 2007

[188] Under the 1994 *Treaty of Accession* Sweden must join the eurozone once it meets the criteria. Sweden maintains that joining the ERM II (a requirement for euro adoption) is voluntary, giving Sweden a de facto opt- out. All political parties have pledged not to join the eurozone without a referendum in favour of doing so. The European Commission appears to have accepted this (see Summary of hearing of Olli Rehn, Economic and Monetary Affairs, 12 January 2010).

[189] Nicolai von Ondarza, Strengthening the Core or Splitting Europe? Prospects and Pitfalls of a Strategy of Differentiated Integration, 2013, *German Institute for International and Security Affairs.*

[190] At which the Government vetoed the proposed EU fiscal compact as a Treaty amendment, resulting in the majority of other Member States proceeding with an intergovernmental treaty without the UK.

[191] HC Deb 8 December 2011 c 197WH

[192] "France and Germany – Together for a stronger Europe of Stability and Growth".

[193] Towards a Deep and Genuine Economic and Monetary Union. The introduction of a Convergence and Competitiveness Instrument, 20 March 2013, COM(2013) 165 final.

[194] Head of European Council on Foreign Relations, Warsaw office.

The European Union: A Democratic Institution? 153

[195] *European Council on Foreign Relations*, September 2013.
[196] The Role of National Parliaments in the European Union, 24 March 2014.
[197] *Open Europe*, Repatriating EU social policy: The best choice for jobs and growth? November 2011, Stephen Booth, Mats Persson and Vincenzo Scarpetta.
[198] Written evidence, 14 October 2013.
[199] Uncorrected evidence, 22 October 2013.
[200] *Open Europe* blog, 1 November 2013
[201] Lords European Union Committee, The Role of the National Parliaments in the European Union, 24 March 2014, chapter 3: Dialogue with the European Commission.
[202] Both of Europa-Institut, Saarland University.
[203] IPEX note
[204] *Journal of Common Market Studies* 2006 Vol 44 Number 3. pp. 533–62, Andreas Follesdal and Simon Hix, "Why There is a Democratic Deficit in the EU: A Response to Majone and Moravcsik".
[205] This charge was explored in a judgment on 18 July 2005 by the Second Senate of the German Constitutional Court. The Court declared void the German *European Arrest Warrant Act* (*Europäisches Haftbefehlsgesetz*). The complainant argued that the Act and the Framework Decision lacked democratic legitimisation by an act of the German Parliament. Judge Lübbe Wolff underlined the need for better *Bundestag* control over government behaviour in the Council, especially where unanimity was required.
[206] Uncorrected evidence, 9 January 2014
[207] Written evidence, 27 September 2013
[208] Uncorrected evidence, 9 January 2014
[209] Uncorrected evidence, 22 October 2013.
[210] Written evidence to Lords EU Committee report, Role of National Parliaments in the European Union, September 2013
[211] EP relations with national parliaments website
[212] From Talking Shop to Working Forum: the evolution of COSAC, 2006.
[213] Presidency Conclusions, 16-17 October 2013.
[214] Uncorrected evidence, 9 January 2014
[215] Research Fellow, Istituto Affari Internazionali
[216] National Parliaments after the Lisbon Treaty: A New Power Player or Mr. No in the EU Decision Making? *Istituto Affari Internazionali* (IAI), *Democracy in the EU after the Lisbon Treaty*, Edited by Raffaello Matarazzo, *Istituto Affari Internazionali* (Rome), *Centro Studi sul Federalismo* (Turin), Notre Europe (Paris).
[217] *Open Democracy*, The European parliament: problem, and solution, Anand Menon, 5 June 2009.
[218] Summarised from "Beyond the European Parliament: Rethinking the EU's democratic legitimacy", 2010.
[219] Ibid, HC Deb 16 July 2013 c181WH; He reiterated these points in the second reading debate on the *European Union (Referendum) Bill* on 5 July 2013.
[220] HC Deb, 30 Jan 2013 c 921.
[221] For further information on the 2011 legislation, see Research Paper 10/79, *The European Union Bill* HC Bill 106 of 2010-11, 2 December 2010.
[222] Reports to date are available at https://www.gov.uk/review-of-the-balance-of-competences.
[223] ESC 24th Report, Reforming the European Scrutiny System in the House of Commons, 28 November 2013.
[224] See HC Deb 12 December 2012 c 291 and HC Deb 17 December 2012 c 569.
[225] Fresh Start Project Mandate for Reform "Securing the Right Deal for the UK: Equipping the EU for a Globalised World", November 2013
[226] European Committee B, Relations Between the European Commission and National Parliaments, 30 January 2014.
[227] ESC Reforming the European Scrutiny System in the House of Commons, 28 November 2013

[228] See *Telegraph*, 11 January 2014

[229] *European Voice*, 16 May 2007.

[230] Anthony Browne and Mats Persson, The case for European localism, September 2011.

[231] Testing European legislation for subsidiarity and proportionality – Dutch list of points for action, 21 June 2013 RESEARCH PAPER 14/25

[232] CER bulletin 91, August-September 2013.

[233] See Foreign Affairs Committee Written evidence from Frank Vibert, LSE, June 2013.

[234] Reforming the European Scrutiny System in the House of Commons, 4 December 2013

[235] Liddle, p 222

[236] Liddle, p 223

[237] *European Voice*, 16 January 2014.

[238] Introduction to The Federal vision, Levels of Governance, and Legitimacy and Levels of Governance in the United States and the European Union, September 2001.

[239] Laurent Pech, *The Institutional Development of the EU Post-Lisbon: A case of plus ça change...?* UCD Dublin European Institute Working Paper 11-5, December 2011. The idea of "double impulse" is borrowed from J. Peterson and M. Shackleton (eds.), *The Institutions of the European Union*, 2006.

INDEX

#

20th century, 56
21st century, 139

A

access, 12, 43, 53, 67, 97, 98, 126
accountability, 6, 25, 41, 57, 58, 63, 69, 71, 80, 99, 101, 102, 109, 116, 122, 127, 132, 133, 135, 137, 138, 146, 151
accounting, 47
acquis communautaire, 114
activism, 68
adjustment, 75
Afghanistan, 12, 17
Africa, 12
agencies, ix, 18, 24, 44
agriculture, 3, 4, 6, 26, 27, 28, 85, 111, 126
air carriers, 47
Al Qaeda, 13
Al Qaeda cells, 13
Albania, 10, 21
ambivalence, 62
Amsterdam Treaty, 27, 66, 120, 125, 143
apathy, 93
appetite, 125
appointees, 121
appointments, 72
appropriations, 48

Aristotle, 55
arrest, 13
Asia, 18
aspiration, 122
assertiveness, 41
assessment, 61
assets, 11, 12
asylum, 13
attachment, 83
attitudes, 89, 91
Austria, 9, 16, 20, 21, 32, 35, 47, 108, 112, 139
authoritarianism, 54
authority(s), viii, 3, 6, 23, 25, 26, 27, 28, 40, 43, 57, 65, 67, 75, 76, 78, 113, 140, 144, 148, 151
autonomy, 74, 82
awareness, 32, 69

B

bad behavior, 96
baggage, 55
bail, 8, 9
Balkans, 10, 11, 12, 17
bankers, 110, 119
banking, 8, 110
banks, 7, 8
bargaining, 98
barriers, 19, 20

156 Index

base, 112, 119
Belgium, 6, 9, 20, 21, 39, 42, 47, 87, 112
benchmarking, 114
beneficiaries, 63
benefits, 42, 77, 78, 95, 113
black market, 141
bond market, 8
bonds, 8
border control, 13
Bosnia, 10
Bosnia-Herzegovina, 10
Brazil, 20
Britain, 74, 131, 133, 139, 141, 146, 152
budget deficit, 8
Bulgaria, 9, 20, 47, 149
bureaucracy, 126
Burundi, 145
businesses, 7, 45

C

Cabinet, 17
candidates, 10, 30, 94, 97, 112
capital markets, 8
carbon, 96
carbon emissions, 96
case law, 73, 75
cash, 8, 42
casting, 92
Caucasus, 12
censorship, 149
central bank, 7
centralisation, 82
CFSP, 1, 3, 10, 11, 126, 130
challenges, 16, 17, 18, 41, 62, 73, 86
checks and balances, 54, 55, 57, 78, 82, 146
children, 55
China, 20, 39, 40, 149
CIA, 38
city(s), 40, 42, 75, 105
citizens, viii, 2, 5, 10, 13, 16, 23, 24, 25, 31,
    44, 52, 53, 54, 57, 66, 67, 69, 77, 79, 81,
    86, 89, 91, 92, 93, 95, 96, 105, 106, 107,
    110, 149, 150
citizenship, 31, 66, 92, 105, 106, 151

Civic Democratic Party, 35
civil liberties, 44, 45
civil servants, 39, 99
civil society, 69, 81, 82, 102, 103, 107, 108,
    111
civil war, 18
climate, 2, 21
climate change, 2
coal, 3
Cold War, 17, 60
color, 15
commercial, 19
common agricultural policy, vii, 1, 3
Common Foreign and Security Policy, 1, 3,
    10, 126
common law, 75
Common Market, 147, 151, 153
communism, 34
communist countries, 9
Communist Party, 35
community(s), 60
compatibility, 64, 143
competition, 13, 71, 130
competitiveness, 115
compilation, 116
complement, 69, 106
complexity, 101
compliance, 67, 71, 76, 80, 148
composition, viii, 24, 26, 32, 77, 84
conception, 52, 54, 142
conciliation, 28
conference, 127, 136, 149, 151
confidentiality, 97
conflict, 18, 73, 75, 129, 145
Congress, vii, ix, 1, 2, 21, 24, 38, 46, 47, 49,
    121
consciousness, 105
consensus, 2, 4, 6, 10, 11, 13, 14, 33, 34, 60,
    98, 99, 103, 119, 127
consent, 15, 21, 27, 29, 30, 40, 46, 47, 76,
    77, 80
constituents, 61
Constitution, 48, 64, 135, 143, 148, 151
constitutional law, 75, 76, 148
constitutional principles, 75

Index

157

construction, 106
consulting, 107, 123
controversial, 43, 59, 94
convention, 141, 148
conviction, 135
cooperation, vii, ix, 1, 2, 6, 12, 13, 17, 18,
  19, 20, 24, 27, 40, 45, 46, 59, 62, 63, 70,
  77, 81, 85, 114, 121, 124, 125, 128, 129,
  131, 134, 136
coordination, 9, 12, 47, 127, 134
corporate governance, 47
corrosion, 151
corruption, 31
cosmopolitanism, 63
cost, 84, 137
Council of Europe, 148
Council of Ministers, viii, 2, 4, 5, 6, 11, 13,
  14, 17, 23, 25, 26, 27, 28, 30, 38, 39, 40,
  41, 43, 72, 78, 95, 119
Council of the European Union, viii, 2, 4,
  23, 25, 26
counterterrorism, 17, 18, 43
covering, 114
credentials, vii, ix, 51, 61, 64, 75, 86, 95,
  96, 128
crimes, 13
crises, 11
crisis management, 11, 12
criticism, 52, 71, 110
Croatia, 9, 20, 47, 104, 149
culture, 10
currency, 1, 3, 61
customer data, 44
cybersecurity, 18
Cyprus, 8, 9, 12, 20, 21, 31, 47, 92
Czech Republic, 9, 20, 35, 47, 92, 93, 108,
  114, 139, 141, 150

deficiency(s), 61, 83
deficit, ix, 16, 51, 54, 66, 71, 72, 77, 81, 82,
  85, 96, 98, 104, 107, 109, 110, 111, 118,
  121, 122, 123, 125, 132, 140, 143, 144
delegates, 84, 125
democrat(s), 35, 62, 63, 105, 128
democratic government, ix, 51
Democratic Party, 35
democratisation, 54, 65
democratization, 76
Denmark, 9, 13, 15, 20, 32, 47, 93, 108,
  112, 114
depth, 44, 63
detention, 38
developing countries, 20
development assistance, 111
deviation, 78
dialogues, 16, 46, 81, 149
diplomacy, 10
direct investment, 19
direct taxation, 93
directives, 14, 74
directors, 26
discrimination, 46, 106
dissatisfaction, 111
distribution, 78
diversity, 40, 78, 82, 133
Doha, 20
domestic issues, 93
domestic laws, 73
domestic policy, 121
dominance, 83
draft, 6, 15, 29, 38, 40, 70, 71, 98, 104, 107,
  120, 128
dream, 142
drug trafficking, 13

E

early warning, 123, 135, 136, 147
Eastern Europe, vii, 1, 9, 37, 139
Economic and Monetary Union, 7, 109,
  110, 114, 152
economic crisis, 94
economic downturn, 19, 32

D

danger, 57
data transfer, 18, 45
decision-making process, 2, 3, 5, 41, 53, 67,
  81, 84, 95, 98, 112, 119, 120, 126, 151
defence, 100, 125

158 Index

economic globalisation, 62
economic growth, 8, 19, 20, 37, 45
economic integration, 109, 142, 143
economic partnership, vii, 1, 2, 24
economic policy, 109
economic reform, 115
economic relations, 19, 44
economic union, 140
economics, 3
ECSC, 74, 149
education, 3, 28, 38, 93
election, 30, 31, 35, 38, 55, 71, 83, 87, 88, 89, 94, 95, 97, 106, 131, 133, 140, 144, 152
embargo, 40
emergency, 8, 13, 104
employers, 107
empowerment, 63
EMU, 7, 109, 114
encouragement, 142
endangered, 46
enemies, 55
energy, 3, 4, 18, 26
energy security, 18
enforcement, 45
enlargement, 9, 10, 15, 95
environment, 3, 27, 34, 35, 38, 45
environmental policy, 3
EP delegations, viii, 24
equality, 34, 56, 59, 78, 82, 144
equilibrium, 111
ESDP, 11, 21
Estonia, 9, 20, 21, 31, 47, 92
EU candidate countries, 127
EU enlargement, 10, 37, 104
European Central Bank, 5, 7, 108, 123
European citizens, viii, 18, 24, 31, 86, 92, 105
European Commission, viii, 2, 4, 6, 11, 14, 17, 21, 23, 25, 26, 29, 30, 31, 39, 41, 43, 44, 45, 52, 67, 69, 78, 79, 119, 149, 152, 153
European Community, 3, 9, 150, 151
European continent, vii, 1, 74
European Court of Justice, 78

European integration, 2, 3, 17, 25, 35, 66, 109, 122, 143
European Security and Defense Policy, 11
Europeanisation, 73, 122
evidence, 73, 81, 83, 86, 92, 99, 113, 116, 117, 118, 120, 122, 123, 124, 125, 134, 136, 146, 147, 150, 152, 153, 154
evolution, 59, 142, 153
executive branch, 78
executive power, 72, 79, 121
exercise, 14, 34, 57, 62, 76, 77, 125, 144
expenditures, 28
expertise, 14
exports, 19, 20

F

fairness, 117
faith, 37, 58
far right, viii, 24, 32
farmers, 107
FAS, 151
fear(s), 10, 15, 16, 32, 42, 83, 97, 118
Federal Government, 144
federalism, 65, 115, 147
filters, 78
financial, 5, 8, 16, 17, 19, 20, 26, 29, 31, 32, 34, 38, 42, 43, 48, 56, 63, 64, 92, 109, 114, 115, 123, 151
financial crisis, 8, 20, 32, 34, 56, 64, 92, 109
financial data, 43
financial institutions, 19
financial markets, 8, 17, 20, 63
financial support, 115
Finland, 9, 16, 20, 21, 32, 47, 139
fiscal policy, 7
flaws, 93, 96
flexibility, 114
flight, 43
flights, 38, 43
food, 19
food products, 19
force, viii, ix, 2, 5, 9, 11, 12, 14, 15, 20, 21, 23, 24, 26, 28, 30, 42, 43, 45, 47, 54, 55, 64, 67, 112, 125, 130, 132, 134, 135

Index   159

foreign affairs, 38
foreign aid, 11
foreign assistance, 6
foreign direct investment, 14
foreign policy, viii, 2, 6, 10, 11, 16, 17, 23, 26, 27, 40
formation, 17, 36
foundations, 53, 116
France, 9, 16, 18, 20, 21, 32, 35, 36, 39, 42, 44, 47, 80, 94, 109, 112, 148, 150, 152
free trade, 20, 138
freedom, 16, 70, 121
funding, 28, 32, 80
funds, 12

G

Georgia, 10
Germany, 9, 20, 21, 31, 35, 47, 94, 100, 108, 109, 110, 112, 124, 139, 141, 143, 144, 145, 147, 152
global trade, 20
globalization, 16, 32
goods and services, 111
governance, 69, 76, 82, 93, 106, 109, 110, 112, 115, 117, 122, 140, 147, 149, 151
government spending, 94
governments, viii, 2, 4, 6, 8, 9, 23, 26, 52, 53, 57, 61, 62, 66, 69, 70, 72, 80, 86, 92, 104, 105, 111, 112, 115, 117, 118, 120, 121, 122, 123, 128, 129, 130, 131, 139, 142, 143, 151
graph, 89, 91
Greece, 6, 8, 9, 20, 21, 32, 36, 47, 52, 54, 55, 92, 94, 108, 109, 149, 150
greed, 43
gross domestic product, 19
group work, 36
growth, 9, 19, 42, 115, 153
guardian, 26, 78
guidance, 128
guidelines, 114, 124

H

hardliners, 36, 37
health, 93
history, 20, 34, 119
homosexuality, 31
hospitality, 42
host, 42, 56
hostilities, 10
hot spots, 12
hotel, 42
House, 16, 46, 51, 119, 123, 124, 132, 137, 146, 149, 153, 154
House of Representatives, 16
human, 34, 38, 40, 54, 57, 60, 70, 147
human right(s), 34, 38, 40, 54, 60, 70, 147
Hungary, 9, 20, 32, 35, 36, 47, 141, 149
hybrid, 66, 142

I

Iceland, 10, 21
ideal, 52, 81
identity, 5, 10, 25, 111, 112
ideology, viii, 24, 32, 41
image, 42
imagination, 57
imbalances, 20
IMF, 8, 110
immigration, 6, 13, 16, 27, 32, 36, 37, 85
impact assessment, 14, 123
imports, 19
improvements, 142
impulses, 143
in transition, 60
incompatibility, 59
independence, 35, 57, 78, 80
India, 20, 39, 60
individual rights, 34
individuals, 87, 126
industry, 45
information exchange, 127
infrastructure, 28
initiation, 123

Index

institutional change, 65
institutional reforms, 66
institutionalisation, 62
integration, vii, 1, 3, 4, 9, 10, 15, 34, 35, 36, 37, 62, 63, 64, 65, 68, 72, 82, 94, 95, 109, 114, 116, 117, 121, 129, 133, 136, 141, 142, 152
intellectual property, 14, 45
intellectual property rights, 14, 45
intelligence, ix, 12, 18, 21, 24, 44, 45
interdependence, vii, 1, 3
interest groups, 107, 133, 149
interest rates, 8
interference, 60
International Criminal Court, 146
international law, 59, 60, 73, 75, 76, 77, 114, 149
International Monetary Fund, 8
international standards, 60
international trade, 14, 111
investment, 2, 16, 19, 20
investors, 8, 19
IPR, 45
Iran, 11, 17, 18, 39
Iraq, 11, 18
Ireland, 8, 9, 13, 15, 20, 21, 35, 47, 114, 147, 148
Israel, 39
issues, vii, viii, 1, 2, 3, 4, 6, 11, 12, 13, 15, 16, 17, 18, 20, 24, 25, 27, 33, 38, 40, 41, 45, 46, 47, 56, 72, 89, 90, 92, 102, 110, 112, 124, 130, 132, 146, 149
Italy, 6, 8, 9, 20, 21, 32, 35, 47, 87, 92, 93, 109, 112, 149, 150

J

job creation, 20, 45
judicial power, 78
judiciary, 54
justification, 123

K

Kosovo, 10

L

languages, 40
Latvia, 9, 20, 21, 47, 93, 108, 149
law enforcement, 17, 18, 43, 44, 45
laws, vii, viii, 1, 3, 5, 9, 23, 25, 40, 73, 75, 113, 119, 138, 139, 140
laws and regulations, 9
lead, 18, 41, 74, 79, 102, 113, 118
leadership, 5, 32
Lebanon, 145
legislative power, viii, 5, 23, 27, 52, 78, 82, 84, 100, 143
legislative proposals, 6, 21, 32, 38, 43, 53, 103, 134, 136
liberalism, 56
liberty, 70
light, ix, 20, 24, 43, 47
Lithuania, 9, 20, 47
loans, 8, 9
lobbying, 54, 86

M

Maastricht Treaty, 27, 66, 85, 95, 98, 105, 114, 143
Macedonia, 10
machinery, 148
majority, viii, 3, 4, 5, 6, 13, 14, 16, 19, 23, 27, 28, 30, 33, 34, 37, 40, 41, 43, 52, 54, 55, 56, 58, 72, 73, 77, 78, 80, 83, 85, 86, 93, 95, 97, 98, 103, 104, 105, 107, 108, 136, 144, 145, 152
man, 58
management, 5, 26, 30
manipulation, 63
marginalisation, 56
market economics, 34
market economy, 9
marriage, 56

Index 161

mass, 44, 55
matter, 58, 69, 77, 82, 118, 137, 142
media, 45, 54, 58, 61, 81, 149
Mediterranean, 141
membership, 9, 10, 16, 21, 74, 76, 89, 91,
   92, 94, 110, 127, 131, 132, 137, 139,
   141, 142, 147, 148, 150
membership criteria, 147
MEPs, viii, 5, 6, 18, 21, 23, 24, 25, 31, 32,
   33, 34, 35, 36, 37, 38, 39, 40, 41, 42, 43,
   45, 46, 48, 49, 83, 84, 95, 96, 97, 100,
   103, 117, 118, 119, 128, 129, 131, 132,
   133, 134, 148, 150
middle class, 55
Middle East, 4, 11, 12, 16, 17
military, 11, 12
minorities, 147
missions, 11, 12, 13
mobile phone, 18, 44
mobile telephony, 96
models, 64, 66, 117, 122
momentum, 13
monetary policy, 5, 7
monetary union, 80, 109
Montenegro, 10
multinational companies, 62

N

national income, 28, 48
national interests, 11, 103, 104
national party(s), 35, 83, 94
national policy, 131
National Security Agency, ix, 18, 24, 44
nationality, viii, 5, 24, 32, 41
NATO, 12, 21, 39, 127
negative effects, 103
negotiating, 14, 99, 102, 115, 141
negotiation, 14, 40, 43, 44
Netherlands, 9, 16, 20, 21, 32, 35, 47, 93,
   108, 113, 119, 124, 138, 139, 141, 148
neutral, 41
NGOs, 62, 108
nominee, 30, 31
North Africa, 17

Northern Ireland, 145
Norway, 21
NSA, 44, 45

O

Obama, 18, 19, 43
Obama Administration, 18, 19, 43
OECD, 87
Office of the United States Trade
   Representative, 22
officials, 13, 17, 18, 19, 36, 40, 43, 45, 47,
   97
openness, 58, 97, 98, 100
operations, 11, 12, 18, 42, 44
opinion polls, 53
opportunities, 53, 61, 95, 101, 105, 107, 111
opt out, 13
organ(s), 5, 143
organize, 4, 60, 79
oversight, 15, 30, 41, 52, 58, 116, 122

P

parallel, 138
participants, 7, 46, 81, 100, 102
participatory democracy, 81, 82, 106, 108
Partido Popular, 35
peace, vii, 1, 3, 11, 17, 25, 42, 67
peace process, 11
peacekeeping, 11
penalties, 85
personal relations, 47
personal relationship, 47
PES, 34
platform, 37, 125
pluralism, 76
Poland, 9, 20, 35, 37, 47, 113, 114, 139,
   141, 150
police, 6, 11, 13, 27, 85
policy initiative, 52
policy issues, 6
policy options, 96
political appointments, 41

political democracy, 55, 56
political groups, viii, 24, 30, 32, 34, 37, 38, 39, 83
political ideologies, 56
political leaders, 65, 71, 77, 86
political participation, 105
political party(s), viii, 24, 25, 32, 35, 48, 86, 95, 97, 146, 152
political partnership, vii, 2, 16
political power, 76
political problems, 18
political system, ix, 51, 57, 78, 81, 87
politics, 34, 36, 37, 56, 62, 65, 79, 82, 83, 102, 130, 146, 150
pollution, 38
popular support, 96, 112
population, 5, 31, 55, 58, 81, 91, 94, 104, 105, 107
population size, 31
portfolio, 26, 31
Portugal, 6, 8, 9, 20, 21, 47, 48, 92, 108, 113
positive attitudes, 91
positive relationship, 91
poultry, 19
power relations, 63
prejudice, 124
preservation, 65, 143
presidency, 38, 80, 97
president, 4, 5, 6, 17, 26, 30, 37, 38, 48, 53, 67, 77, 79, 80, 86, 97, 111, 112, 113, 115, 127, 129, 139, 140, 141
prestige, 42
primacy, 68, 72, 75, 138
principles, 16, 59, 66, 68, 70, 71, 76, 109, 111, 125, 133, 146
problem-solving, 77
procurement, 12
project, 2, 3, 17, 37, 63, 66, 150
proliferation, 12, 17, 102
promoter, 129
proportionality, 70, 104, 125, 134, 135, 137, 139, 154
prosperity, vii, 1, 3, 9, 25, 67
protection, 14, 19, 43, 44, 45, 60, 105, 147

public administration, 82
public awareness, 30, 41
public debt, 8
public interest, 82
public opinion, 95, 143
public policy, 93
public service, 146
public support, 16, 82, 140, 142

Q

questioning, 75

R

racism, 13
ratification, 5, 15, 20, 21, 31, 65
reactions, 126
reading, 71, 73, 85, 102, 147, 148, 153
reality, 109, 118
reasoning, 126
recall, 61, 146
recession, 19, 34
recognition, 43, 111, 144
recommendations, 20, 29, 44, 97, 134, 135
reconciliation, 42, 74
reform(s), viii, ix, 2, 5, 11, 16, 21, 23, 25, 32, 45, 47, 51, 53, 61, 80, 82, 83, 86, 105, 109, 111, 112, 115, 125, 127, 130, 139, 140, 141, 142, 143, 150, 153
reformers, 86
regulations, 79, 138, 140
regulatory framework, 19
rejection, 43, 45
relative size, 32
relativity, 52
relevance, 104
rendition, 38
requirements, 36, 60, 111, 119, 144
resolution, 44, 46, 48, 49, 115, 149
resources, 12, 86, 123
response, 17, 18, 19, 20, 42, 44, 46, 55, 61, 76, 91, 106, 109, 152
responsiveness, 113

Index 163

restrictions, 81, 148
retaliation, 14
revenue, 48
rhetoric, 86
rights, 13, 18, 31, 32, 41, 43, 44, 55, 59, 60,
  66, 70, 85, 105, 106, 138, 148, 149
risk(s), 8, 20, 76, 110, 114, 117, 126
Romania, 9, 20, 47, 93, 108, 149
root(s), 34, 36, 93, 95
rule of law, 11, 70, 78, 108, 147
rules, 4, 9, 14, 20, 38, 42, 45, 68, 73, 79, 82,
  97, 99, 103, 104, 105, 109, 114, 116,
  127, 128, 140
Russia, 16, 39, 149

S

safety, 111
sanctions, 9, 10, 18, 148, 149
Sarbanes-Oxley Act, 47
Scandinavia, 139
scatter, 91
science, 93
scope, 14, 27, 54, 79, 100, 111, 113, 130,
  134, 135, 137, 141, 142
SEA, 104
Second World, 56, 145
security, 2, 3, 11, 13, 21, 38, 44, 55, 70,
  100, 121, 125
Senate, 31, 46, 122, 130, 140, 153
Serbia, 10
services, 14, 40, 45
shape, 29, 34, 56, 64, 86, 94
showing, 87, 89, 92, 100
signals, 44, 112
signs, 31
single currency, 7, 16
Single European Act, 27, 72, 85, 98, 104
single market, vii, 1, 3, 79, 103, 104, 114,
  138
slaves, 54
Slovakia, 9, 20, 21, 47, 141
social group, 107, 145
social policy, 27, 114, 153
social security, 27, 100

society, 52, 55, 56, 61, 63, 82, 107, 109, 112
solidarity, 109, 115
solution, 62, 63, 103, 114, 116, 118, 130,
  150, 151, 153
sovereign countries, vii, 1
sovereign state, 59, 64
sovereignty, 2, 3, 6, 10, 13, 15, 16, 32, 35,
  57, 58, 59, 60, 62, 63, 65, 72, 73, 74, 75,
  76, 109, 110, 141, 142, 146, 148
Spain, 8, 9, 18, 20, 21, 35, 44, 47, 92, 109,
  113, 150
Spanish Constitution, 148
species, 65
speech, 45, 86, 133, 139, 140
spending, 7, 28, 29, 82, 93, 94, 110
Spring, 17
stability, vii, 1, 9, 16, 17, 19, 20, 65, 66, 147
staffing, 41
stakeholders, 115
State of the Union address, 149
statutes, 75
steel, 3
stock, 19
stress, 18, 54, 115
stroke, 130
structural funds, 80
structural reforms, 115
structure, 65, 77, 78, 109, 116, 121, 133,
  142
style, 31, 138
supervisor, 8
Supreme Court, 148
surplus, 9
surveillance, ix, 2, 18, 24, 44, 45, 109, 116
Sweden, 9, 15, 16, 20, 21, 32, 47, 139, 141,
  152
symbolism, 42
Syria, 18, 149

T

tanks, 133
tariff, 14, 19, 20
tax matters, viii, 23
taxation, 5, 7, 26, 100, 110

164 Index

taxes, 106, 110
taxpayers, 151
technical support, 39
techniques, 62
tension(s), 2, 9, 12, 15, 18, 19, 47, 62
terrorism, viii, 6, 12, 13, 17, 24, 38, 42, 43
terrorist attack, 13, 43
theatre, 97
thinning, 140
tobacco, 147
top-down, 110
trade, vii, viii, 1, 2, 3, 4, 8, 14, 15, 16, 17,
    19, 20, 21, 23, 25, 26, 27, 40, 45, 85,
    107, 151
trade agreement, 14, 15, 21, 27
trade deficit, 8
trade policy, vii, 1, 3, 14, 17
trade union, 107
trading bloc, 14
trading partners, 2, 17
traditions, 36, 107
training, 11
transformations, 62
translation, 40, 81
transparency, 2, 5, 25, 42, 53, 58, 67, 71, 72,
    97, 98, 99, 100, 101, 111, 120, 123, 129,
    141, 146, 151
treaties, vii, 1, 2, 4, 20, 25, 26, 73, 78, 112,
    132, 137
treatment, 78
Treaty of Amsterdam, 106
Treaty of Nice, 66
Treaty of Rome, 74, 77, 107, 151
Treaty on European Union, 68, 151
Turkey, 10, 12, 21
turnout, 30, 31, 41, 52, 85, 87, 88, 89, 90,
    91, 92, 93, 94, 97, 146, 150

U

U.S. policy, 18, 19
U.S.-EU relations, vii, ix, 2, 18, 19, 24, 42
Ukraine, 10
unions, 54, 61
unit of account, 7

United, 2, 6, 9, 12, 13, 16, 17, 18, 19, 20,
    21, 22, 32, 33, 34, 35, 39, 42, 43, 44, 45,
    46, 47, 48, 51, 59, 65, 100, 102, 111,
    130, 140, 145, 147, 149, 154
United Nations (UN), 59, 65, 148, 149
United States, 2, 12, 13, 16, 17, 18, 19, 20,
    21, 22, 39, 42, 43, 44, 45, 46, 47, 65,
    100, 111, 130, 140, 145, 147, 154

V

value added tax, 48
variations, 114
VAT, 48
vehicles, 63
venue, 37, 46
veto, 3, 40, 43, 52, 53, 72, 82, 85, 96, 103,
    105, 121, 135, 136, 137, 138, 141
Vice President, 6, 140
violence, 145
vision(s), 55, 62, 122, 133, 147, 154
vote, 6, 29, 30, 31, 33, 34, 37, 39, 40, 41,
    42, 43, 45, 55, 79, 80, 83, 85, 86, 87, 89,
    92, 95, 98, 99, 102, 105, 106, 117, 129
voters, 34, 41, 61, 72, 83, 86, 92, 94, 96,
    112, 121, 130, 132, 140, 150
voting, 3, 4, 5, 6, 13, 14, 15, 27, 30, 32, 33,
    37, 41, 52, 54, 57, 59, 72, 73, 78, 86, 87,
    92, 93, 95, 98, 103, 104, 105, 106, 121,
    130

W

war, vii, 1, 3, 11, 74, 152
Washington, 17, 21, 46, 48, 49
weakness, 52, 85
wealth, 52, 56
weapons, 12, 17
web, 145
weblog, 109
websites, 81
welfare, 93
Western Europe, vii, 1, 146
White Paper, 66, 78, 107

wholesale, 37
withdrawal, 35
workers, 19
working class, 55
working groups, 98, 99, 121
workload, 84
World Bank, 59
World War I, vii, 1, 3, 59, 77
worldwide, 45
worry, ix, 13, 18, 24, 44, 83

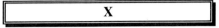

xenophobia, 13

Yale University, 105
young people, 94